NATIONS
CHURCH OF THE

**BECOMING A
FIRST CENTURY CHURCH**
in a 21st Century World

MIKE ATKINS

ACKNOWLEDGEMENTS

I give thanks to the Lord.

To all who have contributed to the growth and development of helping me to understand God's Heart for the Nations, whose names would fill these pages. Your names will not be forgotten though to numerous to mention here. And, in memory of Dr. M.G. McLuhan Pastor, Writer, Missionary, Statesman, Teacher, Scholar and Friend who took the time to mentor a young man into a lifelong love for the Word of God.

To my most important "nation":
my treasured gifts from the Father;
Patty, Micah, Rebekah
and Sarah Ann.
Thank you for journeying with me to
the nations for Christ.

Church of the Nations
Becoming A 1st Century Church in a 21st Century World
Mike Atkins

Church of the Nations – Becoming A 1st Century Church in a 21st Century World
Copyright @ 1995, 2007 Mike Atkins, Church of the Nations, Athens, Georgia

Requests for information should be addressed to Mike Atkins Teaching Ministries International
3205 West Big Trails Drive, Jackson, Wyoming 83001
www.mikeatkinsministry.com
1-866-733-4032
matmi@bresnan.net

Printed in the United States
ISBN: 0-9759218-9-4
ISBN 13: 978-0-9759218-9-0

Printed in the USA by
Morris Publishing
3212 E. Hwy 30 ● Kearney, NE 68847

CONTENTS

As with so many things in life, there comes a time in writing that one must simply put pen to paper, and begin. The result is rarely the stirring, world-changing masterpiece hoped for, but, at least, finally it's out.

Those who first heard these thoughts and passions expressed over a cup of coffee or from a pulpit can now sit down and scrutinize them on the written page. Divorced from my particular brand of persuasion, the ideas must stand alone. This will prove their validity — or their demise.

This, I think, is the reason for so many unwritten or half-finished books. Verbal communication allows the occasional "that's not what I meant," or the opportunity to change tactics when the listener raises an eyebrow.

Writing gives no second chance.

Beyond my selfish desire to have communicated well, however, is my greater desire to have said something that needed to be said. If these words stir up something of the spirit of Paul the apostle, whose ambition it was to . . .

"Preach the gospel where Christ was not known, so that I would not be building on someone else's foundation." [1]

...then I've accomplished my goal.

The Church is called to be a healing center and a teaching center, without question. But with a greater mission in mind: To awaken to our calling to be thrust out into the world as ministers of reconciliation, calling men to Christ, and calling them everywhere.

To this end I write and unto this end I live: That men everywhere may know Christ and His resurrection power, having the promise of salvation and the hope of eternal life.

May the Church of Jesus Christ become truly a Church of the Nations.

ENDNOTES

1   Romans 15:20

What is a Church of the Nations?

Stated simply, a Church of the Nations is a body of believers made up of people from every manner of background, dedicated to people of every manner of background.

It's the body of Christ reaching out to every nation — in as real and genuine a way as we saw in the first century.

A Church of the Nations is dedicated to two propositions: First, that the good news of Jesus Christ is for every man, woman and child — regardless of ethnic, racial, socio-economic, educational or professional status. Second, that the body of Christ has a mission to take the good news to every part of the world where the name of Jesus is as yet unknown.

As a single, local church, we are limited in the role any of us can play. But we should be committed to being a church that is locally igniting, regionally impacting and globally influencing.

To this end, a Church of the Nations seeks, deliberately, to awaken the individual giftedness of each member. As the apostle Paul reminded us, the goal of leadership is to:

"Prepare God's people for works of service, so that the Body of Christ may be built up."[1]

This happens when:

"The whole body, joined and held together by every supporting ligament, grows and builds itself up in love, as each part does its work."[2]

A Church of the Nations requires not the superhuman efforts of a few — but the dedicated efforts of the many. Each member of the body of Christ has a part to play. Each person helps to advance or to detract from the mission of the church.

Again, no single person or church can accomplish the goal. But a unified force of God's people, working toward a common purpose in love, have a great influence in the realm of the Spirit. So much that, according to Christ Himself,

"The gates of hell will not prevail against it.."[3]

It's my prayer that as you read the words that follow, you will seek the Father's heart about your place in this vision. May the Father's heart for the nations fill your own heart, and may the Church of Jesus Christ truly become, as she was destined to be, a Church of the Nations.

ENDNOTES

1   Ephesians 4:12

2   Ephesians 4:16

3   Mathew 16:18

CHAPTER

1

Defining the Nations

•••

A nation is found anywhere that people with a common culture, common needs and a common language gather together as a distinct group.

What is a Nation? Christ commanded his Church to make disciples of all nations, but how do we define a nation? How do we measure the success or failure of the Church in regard to this historic mandate? Are we fulfilling Christ's commission?

The newspaper headlines and television reporters are broadcasting a message to the Church. The message is profoundly important: We must redefine our concept of nations.

DEFINING BY THE BOOK

There are two words in the original languages of the Bible that define the concept of nations. The word used in Hebrew is: *gowy* {pronounced: go'-ee} and means nation or people. The word used in Greek is: *ethnos* {pronounced: eth'-nos} and is defined as:

1) a multitude associated or living together

2) a company, troop, swarm

3) a multitude of individuals of the same nature or genus

4) the human race

5) a race, nation, people group

None of these definitions requires a geographic boundary drawn on a map. The ethnos or "nations" of the world are simply companies of individual people, associated or living together, who are of the same nature or people group.

THE INTERNATIONAL SCENE

The once powerful Soviet Union has become a mish-mash of independent republics with unpronounceable names. The now extinct Yugoslavia has been redefined as Croatia, Bosnia and Serbia; yet no one can show us where one ends and the other begins. Our inner cities have been renamed the "fourth-world" and our universities have become centers of an extraordinarily diverse multi-culturalism. We must recognize the obvious fact: *nations can no longer be defined as geographic countries drawn on a map.*

A nation is found anywhere that people with a common culture, common needs and a common language gather together as a distinct group.

THE NATIONS AROUND US

The nations are no longer over there somewhere — across the ocean or on a different continent. The nations of the earth are intertwined — they are all around us.

They are at our shopping malls and in our school corridors. They are walking on the streets of our cities and they are lobbying on the steps of our capitols. They are our next-door-neighbors and our corporate chiefs. The nations of the world are in our back yard!

They are from Pakistan and Indonesia, Europe and The Middle East. But they are also from Boston and Chicago, Atlanta and Los Angeles. They are African-Americans and Native-Americans, first generation immigrants and Daughters of the American Revolution. They are the young and the old — the rich and the poor. They are our co-workers and our in-laws! They — are us!

The nations are not countries — they are people — wherever they reside geographically — who view themselves as being distinct in some way from the other people around them and who have found others like themselves with whom to relate and interact.

THE NATION OF ROCK AND ROLL?

Whether it is the millions across the globe known as "Rock and Rollers", or those with the "pin-striped suits of Wall Street" in New York's financial district, our concept of nations must be redefined to keep pace with the accelerating melt-down of our former ways of identifying boundaries.

A businessman in Cairo may have more in common with a businessman from Hong Kong than he does with a street kid from his own city. Even though their geographic locations are closer in proximity, their human experiences are further apart than the North and South poles. And the potential for meaningful interaction and effective dialogue between any two individuals is almost entirely dependent upon their capacity to speak one another's "language," understand one another's culture and relate to one another's needs.

When the Bible commands us to:

"Go and make disciples of all nations, baptizing them in the name of the Father and of the Son and of the Holy Spirit" [1]

It is no longer necessary for us to think exclusively of jumping on the next plane and heading to some far away country. We will find the nations playing with our children at the park, or playing golf at the annual tournament. If we have eyes to see by the Spirit we will find that the nations of the earth have come to us — and the fields are truly ripe unto harvest!

A NEW WAY OF SEEING

For example: If we define the nations as God defines them we can think in terms of the nomadic Kurds of northern Iraq —an obvious "nation within a nation." But, we can similarly think in terms of the freshman class of the University of Georgia. Both represent a nation — a group of people with a set of shared human experiences — existing within a larger identifiable community.

Among the tribal Kurdish people we could further identify "nations" as the handicapped, the children, single adults or the elderly. Likewise within the freshman class we can find the foreign students or the married students, the athletes or the druggies.

Each of these sub-sets of young adults have even further and more defined cultures, needs and languages. We need people who understand these cultures and are led by the Holy Spirit to penetrate them with the life-giving reality of Jesus Christ.

A LESSON FROM ISRAEL

An excellent biblical example is Israel. God declared Israel a nation before He ever gave them a land to inhabit. Even then the land God gave them was divided into tribal nations. Later the tribe of Judah became a separate nation-state. Eventually Israel lost their land and were scattered among the other countries, yet, they never lost their distinctiveness as a people. Likewise the Levites were a kind of "nation within a nation" in that they had no physical inheritance in the land. They were bound together only by their common ancestry and calling. Israel was a nation of nations that were united as a country.

MAKING A STRATEGIC DISTINCTION

It is this distinction between the *countries* and *nations* that must be made or we will miss the significance of Christ's call to the Church and confuse our strategic objective as the people of God.

We are called to be a Church of the Nations. We are called to people — wherever they physically live. We cannot measure our progress by lines on a map. We can only mark our progress one human heart at a time — as each one turns from death to life in Jesus' name.

Because of the amazing diversity, no one church or person can minister to all of the nations alone. But a committed fellowship of believers — each reaching out to the various nations around them as the Spirit of God individually leads them — can be a powerful tool in the Father's plan.

A NEW VISION FOR THE LOCAL CHURCH

We must see the local church as an *embassy*. Each member of the congregation must see themselves as *ambassadors* and the leadership of the Church must view themselves as *equippers* who are commissioned of God to awaken, resource, train and send the Church unto the nations to which they are called. It is this strategic aim to which this book is devoted.

The Church must cease being a place of comfortable religion and rise up again to her calling and mandate. We gather together to be healed, filled and empowered — that we might go as Christ's emissaries to the nations.

When we lose the mission — we've lost the whole point of the gathering. Church becomes a dry, social - intellectual exercise with no sense of destiny or goal.

Depending on our particular brand of faith, we either become wrapped up in the emotions of spirit-filled ecstasy or dry up in the dustiness of a dead formalism. We analyze the issues or fill up with the spirit but we never solve the problems or pour out the anointing.

We don't need to lose our intellectual analysis nor quench the Holy Spirit's fire. What we do need is to reunite it all to the sense of mission which has driven the Church since the days of the apostles — to take the good news of Jesus Christ to the lost — and lead them to Christ! We must recover the great adventure of the kingdom of God — reaching all nations with the life-changing story of God's love — until every tribe and nation and kindred and tongue have heard.

RECOVERING THE MISSION

It is critical that we stop viewing the Church and her mission as a minor sub-plot to the theme of the human race. The mission of the Church is *the* theme of all of human history. All of mankind is caught up in the storyline and the eternal fate of every man, woman and child is being written into it's pages.

It is critical that the Church recover her calling to the nations. We are entering an era in human history when the geographic lines on the globe will no longer be adequate to define where the nations begin and end. Even here in North America the Canadians barely defeated a referendum to become two separate states of Canada and Quebec. Who's to say that the same thing may not happen some day in the United States of America?

TRACKING THE TRENDS

A recent U.S. News and World Report[2] study predicted that (present trends continuing) by the year 2095 the U.S. population will be 50% Non-European which means 1 out of 2 people will be from a culture and language group very different from the white, Anglo-Saxon, protestant heritage which has been the majority in America for centuries.

We are seeing the growing unrest emerging from the diversity of cultures which are trying to find expression in our 21st century techno-world. If the Church is to be prepared for the future, we must start now to recognize that the task is beyond the reach of the pastor and his leadership.

The man and woman in the pew must be equipped to reach out, in the Name of Christ, unto the nations — in our cities and around the world. This is the age for the individual believer to be equipped, trained, empowered by the Holy Spirit and sent out into the harvest field.

The task is beyond the reach of the pulpit — it is by the hands of those in the pew that the harvest will be gathered in the days ahead — or left in the field untouched.

A RETURN TO THE MANDATE

A Church of the Nations is a church that recognizes the harvest field around them and has taken seriously Christ's call to *"become all things to all men so that by all means we might win some"*.[3]

Their discipleship, education, fellowship and worship all point to the ultimate goal which is the awakening of the saints of God to their high and holy calling as ambassadors to the nations on behalf of Christ.

What is a Nation? It is any group of people with common needs and a common culture, who speak a common language and who see themselves as distinct from other groups of people around them.

What is a Church of the Nations? It is any church that begins to look beyond their own self-interest to awaken their people to go to the nations around them with the life-giving story of Jesus Christ. It is any local church that arises to her calling to leave the comfort zone of safety and fellowship to go into the battle for the souls of men.

May the Church respond to this pivotal moment in human history and go to the nations lifting high the banner of Christ!

ENDNOTES

1 Matthew 28:19

2 U.S. News and World Report; October 30, 1995; Face of the Nation Titled, Ahead: A Mostly Minority America; pg. 23 Data from U.S. Census Bureau.

3 1 Corinthians 9:22

CHAPTER

2

Setting the Stage

•••

God's heart has always been for the nations because the nations are about people — Human beings, lost but loved by the Father—

We all grow up in different worlds. Men grow up in one world. Women in another. Blacks grow up in a different world from whites. The wealthy experience one kind of life. The poor know something entirely different.

The well-educated move in arenas that the less-educated will never know.

There are exceptions to every rule, of course. But the majority of the time, we each seek out the familiar — and then stay there. We learn the rules of conduct, and practice the roles until we can operate comfortably within the circle of relationships we've chosen.

Occasionally we break ranks. We venture on vacation into a different culture. We strike up a conversation with someone from a world different from our own. For a few hours we take a journey into a human experience that is diverse.

Then, just as quickly, we retreat into our own familiar and safe haven — more convinced than ever that it is the best way to live.

The pattern is understandable. We all like to feel comfortable and safe in our surroundings. Different languages and music, different speech patterns and cultural approaches are disorienting and even confusing at times.

Rather than risk being misunderstood, it's easier to relate to those who are like us.

So we live in those neighborhoods. We shop in those shopping districts. We go to those schools which mirror our own culture and style.

But before long, these ties become more than bridges to people of common heritage. They become walls which divide the human family. We have natives and tourists, West and East, members and non-members, contemporary and traditional...and the list goes on.

What is truly disturbing is when these divisions emerge in the one place on earth that was designed to remove them — the Church of the Lord Jesus Christ.

The New Testament Church is the plan of the Master Designer to unify that which He Himself had formerly divided — and display that unity to a world hopelessly searching for peace.

BACK TO THE BEGINNING

The Father created Man with a purpose which, if followed, would have resulted in unbroken fellowship with Himself and other men.

In his pre-fallen condition, man walked with God in the cool of the garden. He walked in complete, unashamed intimacy and honesty. No disharmony existed between man and God or man and woman. Transparency characterized those days of innocence.

But innocence and intimacy soon gave way to rebellion and separation. Man's relationship with his Creator was broken. His relationship with his spouse was severely damaged. Trust and honesty were casualties — and hiding, blaming and running away were introduced.

Man became lonely — separate from God — for the first time in his life. That loneliness has never been completely eliminated.

In fact, as the first nine chapters of Genesis record, this tragic spiral led to the near-total annihilation of man. The last chapter of the human race could have been written right there in the garden.

But Man was given a second chance. Though his condition was fallen and rebellious, God sought a way to preserve His creation for an extended season — until a plan of rescue could be effected.

God judged Man righteously. But through His favor on Noah, He enabled the race to continue.

BEGINNING AGAIN

From the three sons of Noah — Ham, Shem and Japheth — the human family began to grow. Soon, seventy nations of families emerged.[1]

One in language and one in blood, the human race carried tremendous potential. But as always, potential could be used as much for evil as for good.

Soon a chain reaction of rebellion occurred which, as we know, culminated in the tower of Babel. Man attempted to establish his own authority as equal to God's — a serious breach of divine law.

What was the Father's response? In divine judgment, God confounded the language of mankind. He guaranteed the division of the human race into smaller, less threatening groups, each with limited influence.

Even as these bands of like-speaking members began to spread out over the face of the earth, the Father was developing His plan to reunite them again.

Genesis chapter twelve reveals the initial stages of the strategy. Out from among the many nations of the earth, God chose a man. His name was Abram. Seeing his heart of openness, and seeking a partner in His plan, God called Abram out and made a covenant with him.[2]

Look closely at these three chapters of Genesis 10, 11 and 12. They set the stage for all of human history to follow. They are critical to understanding all of God's subsequent dealings with the human race.

GOD'S HEART HAS ALWAYS BEEN FOR THE NATIONS.

Why? Because the nations are not about geographical boundaries. God's heart has always been for the nations because the nations are about people — Human beings, lost but loved by the Father, all descendants of the first man and all of one blood and one common human condition.[3] Confounded in speech and culture, yet all united by our lost relationship with the Creator — our universal need is for a Savior and our deep inner yearning is to be reconciled to the Father.

Through Abraham (whose name means "father of many nations"),[4] God determined to bring forth a new nation whose sole purpose would be to become a light to the other nations and to reveal to them the presence and plan of God.

THE CALLING OF ISRAEL

Israel was not chosen from the other nations because she was more numerous than the others.[5] Nor was she chosen because she was more deserving.

God chose Israel out from among the nations for the same purpose that He chose the Levites from among the other tribes of

Israel. The Levites were chosen to be a tribe of priests who would go to God for Israel and who would go to Israel for God.[6] The Levites were not chosen because God loved them more or because they deserved the special place of priesthood. God needed someone to fulfill a role in His plan, and they were chosen for that purpose.

In the same way, Israel was chosen out from among all the other nations to be a kingdom of priests to and for the nations.[7] Israel's only reason for existence was to fulfill God's call for a people who would minister to the nations for Him. He gave His Word to Israel so that the nations would see Israel's wisdom and prosperity and come, seeking the source of her guidance.[8] He gave His presence to Israel to cause the nations nearby to hear and inquire as to the God of Israel. Even the temple built by Solomon was dedicated to those of any nation who heard of God's great Name and were willing to pray to Him in faith.[9] The Word, the Presence and the Temple were all meant to be testimonies to the nations.

Again, we see that the Father's heart has always been for the nations — for the people of every nation — to know His love, His will and His ways.

By the time Solomon came to the throne of Israel, God's plan was starting to be realized. From a single family in Egypt, the nation of Israel had grown under slavery to over 3 million strong. Delivered by a mighty hand from Egyptian bondage, Israel wandered in the Sinai wilderness 40 years before a new generation who trusted God's Word conquered and possessed the land promised them. Saul was Israel's first king, succeeded by King David and finally Solomon; David's son.

LOSING THEIR WAY

As the Name of the Lord increased in the earth, the nations of the world came to Israel to inquire of Solomon. With the wisdom God gave him, he answered even the most difficult problems.[10] Israel was truly becoming a light to the nations, and the Name of the Lord was beginning to be spread over all the earth.[11]

But a tragic sin by Solomon[12] led to another downward spiral of self-destruction, until Israel was eventually divided into two kingdoms. Within a few short years, Israel had been conquered entirely and the majority of the people scattered into exile. They became slaves among the very nations they had been sent to as light.

Though preserved supernaturally as a remnant, Israel lost her place of esteem and awe among the nations. The Name of the Lord was ridiculed instead of honored.[13] Each nation turned again to their own gods and their own ways, while the hope of uniting people from every tribe and nation and kindred and tongue under the authority of the Lord was seemingly lost forever.

In order to protect Israel from His own judgment upon her sin of idolatry, God brought a form of spiritual blindness upon her. From Isaiah chapter six onward Israel has had a veil over her understanding in regard to the Father's heart for the nations.

Isaiah 6:9-10

He said, "Go and tell this people: " 'Be ever hearing, but never understanding; be ever seeing, but never perceiving.' Make the heart of this people calloused; make their ears dull and close their eyes. Otherwise they might see with their eyes, hear with their ears, understand with their hearts, and turn and be healed."[14]

Israel mistook the blessing of God's Word and His presence as signs of His exclusive love for her. Turning her heart away from the nations, Israel's role of priesthood was completely lost. By the time John the Baptist stood baptizing on the shores of the Jordan river, Israel had come to despise the very nations she had been created to serve as a nation of priests.[15]

In spite of her blindness, the Father, in fulfillment of His promise to Abraham, brought forth through Israel the Savior of the world.

Jesus Christ, the Son of God, came through the lineage of Abraham, Isaac and Jacob.[16] Born of the Virgin Mary by the will of God, He became the perfect lamb of God without spot or blemish,[17] offered as a sinless sacrifice for the rebellion of the whole world.[18] As Jesus sought to reveal the Father's heart to Israel, He was rejected.[19] Crucified and buried, His message of God's love for the whole world seemed to have died with Him.

And then He burst the bonds of Death on the third day, and the world has never been the same.

1   Genesis 10:1-32 All nations listed were descendent of one of the sons of Noah. The Holy
    Spirit led Moses to be very specific to record these descendent nations in detail.

2   Genesis 12:3 "I will bless those who bless you, and whoever curses you I will curse; and all
    peoples on earth will be blessed through you."

3   Acts 17:26 "From one man he made every nation of men that they should inhabit the
    whole earth..."

4   Genesis 17:4-5 especially verse 5b "...your name will be called Abraham, for I have made
    you a father of many nations."

5   Deuteronomy 7:7 " The LORD did not set his affection on you and choose you because you
    were more numerous than other peoples, for you were the fewest of all peoples."

6   Numbers 8:9-11

7   Exodus 19:5b-6 "...out of all nations you will be my treasured possession. Although the
    whole earth is mine, you will be for me a kingdom of priests and a holy nation.' These are
    the words you are to speak to the Israelites."

8   Deuteronomy 4:6-8 Observe them carefully, for this will show your wisdom and under-
    standing to the nations, who will hear about all these decrees and say, "Surely this great
    nation is a wise and understanding people." What other nation is so great as to have their
    gods near them the way the LORD our God is near us whenever we pray to him? And what
    other nation is so great as to have such righteous decrees and laws as this body of laws I
    am setting before you today?

9   1 Kings 8:41-43 "As for the foreigner who does not belong to your people Israel but has
    come from a distant land because of your name — for men will hear of your great name
    and your mighty hand and your outstretched arm — when he comes and prays toward this
    temple, then hear from heaven, your dwelling place, and do whatever the foreigner asks of
    you, so that all the peoples of the earth may know your name and fear you, as do your own
    people Israel, and may know that this house I have built bears your Name."

10 1 Kings 10:1-3 "When the queen of Sheba heard about the fame of Solomon and his rela-
    tion to the name of the LORD, she came to test him with hard questions—she came to
    Solomon and talked with him about all that she had on her mind. Solomon answered all
    her questions; nothing was too hard for the king to explain to her."

11 1 Kings 10:24 "The whole world sought audience with Solomon to hear the wisdom God
    had put in his heart."

12 1 Kings 11:4 "As Solomon grew old, his wives turned his heart after other gods, and his heart was not fully devoted to the LORD his God, as the heart of David his father had been."

13 Ezekiel 36:20 "And wherever they went among the nations they profaned my holy name, for it was said of them, `These are the LORD's people, and yet they had to leave his land."

14 Isaiah 6:9-10 He said, "Go and tell this people: " 'Be ever hearing, but never under-standing; be ever seeing, but never perceiving.' Make the heart of this people calloused; make their ears dull and close their eyes. Otherwise they might see with their eyes, hear with their ears, understand with their hearts, and turn and be healed."

2 Corinthians 3:14-15 But their minds were made dull, for to this day the same veil remains when the old covenant is read. It has not been removed, because only in Christ is it taken away. Even to this day when Moses is read, a veil covers their hearts.

Romans 11:8 as it is written: "God gave them a spirit of stupor, eyes so that they could not see and ears so that they could not hear, to this very day."

15 John 4:9 The Samaritan woman said to him, "You are a Jew and I am a Samaritan woman. How can you ask me for a drink?" (For Jews do not associate with Samaritans.)

16 Matthew 1:1 "A record of the genealogy of Jesus Christ the son of David, the son of Abraham: —"

17 John 1:29 The next day John saw Jesus coming toward him and said, "Look, the Lamb of God, who takes away the sin of the world!

18 1 John 2:2 He is the atoning sacrifice for our sins, and not only for ours but also for the sins of the whole world.

19 John 1:11 "He came to that which was his own, but his own did not receive him."

CHAPTER

3

Renewing the Vision

•••

He is uniting people of every tribe, nation, kindred and tongue not by military might, not by political persuasion, but by a new birth into the family of God.

Jesus' first action as risen Lord was to bring to birth his Church. Made up of Jew and Gentile, slave and free, Greek and Scythian, the Church was charged to:

"...go and make disciples of all nations, baptizing them in the name of the Father and of the Son and of the Holy Spirit, and teaching them to obey everything I have commanded you. And surely I am with you always, to the very end of the age."[1]

He opened their understanding to His plan to unite people from every nation by the body of Christ, the Church.[2] His last recorded words to His people just before his ascension back to heaven were these:

"But you will receive power when the Holy Spirit comes on you; and you will be my witnesses in Jerusalem, and in all Judea and Samaria, and to the ends of the earth."[3]

Within a generation, Paul had established churches in Rome, Galatia, Ephesus, Colossae, Philippi, Corinth, and Thessalonica. There were worshippers in Ethiopia, Antioch, Laodicea, Smyrna and many other regions of the world. Christ's Church, as its enemies in Thessalonica remarked, was turning the world upside down![4]

At the same time that the Roman Empire's unity was unraveling, God was beginning to bring together Hebrews from Israel, Syrians from Antioch, Italians from Rome and Greeks from Athens, Ethiopians from Africa and Turks from Cappadocia, all united in love by the agency of the Holy Spirit.

This same activity is God's work today. He is uniting people of every tribe, nation, kindred and tongue[5] not by military might, not by political persuasion, but by a new birth into the family of God. Though many will continue to reject Him —

Yet to all who received him, to those who believed in his name, he gave the right to become children of God.[6]

Yes, God's heart has always been for the nations. He is honored by the diversity of people gathering in His Name, loving and receiving one another as members of the family of God, purchased by blood[7] and treasured by the Father.

This is a heart of a Church of the Nations. A church for all people. Not a white church. Not a black church. Not a rich church. Not a poor church. Not a church of ambition, but a church whose only ambition is to pursue God, to advance the Kingdom and to build the Church.

A Church of the Nations is a church that rejoices in its diversity because it reflects the heart of her Lord — a heart for all people; a heart for the nations.

ENDNOTES

1   Matthew 12:19b-20 "...go and make disciples of all nations, baptizing them in the name of the Father and of the Son and of the Holy Spirit, and teaching them to obey everything I have commanded you. And surely I am with you always, to the very end of age."

2   Luke 24:45-47 Then he opened their minds so they could understand the Scriptures. He told them, "This is what is written: The Christ will suffer and rise from the dead on the third day, and repentance and forgiveness of sins will be preached in his name to all nations, beginning at Jerusalem.

3   Acts 1:8 "But you will receive power when the Holy Spirit comes on you; and you will be my witness in Jerusalem, and in all Judea and Samaria, and to the ends of the earth."

4   Acts 17:6b " These that have turned the world upside down are come hither also;" (KJV)

5   Revelation 5:9-10 And they sang a new song: "You are worthy to take the scroll and to open its seals, because you were slain, and with your blood you purchased men for God from every tribe and language and people and nation. You have made them to be a kingdom and priests to serve our God, and they will reign on the earth."

6   John 1:12 Yet to all who received him, to those who believed in his name, he gave the right to become children of God.

7   1 Peter 1:18-19 For you know that it was not with perishable things such as silver or gold that you were redeemed — but with the precious blood of Christ, a lamb without blemish or defect.

CHAPTER

4

Pursuing God

•••

To pursue God means more than going to church. To pursue God means to seek out and discover who He is, and what He is doing in your world and to press into it with all your heart.

Have you noticed? There have always been two types of people. Those who pursue God and His glory, and those who ignore God and pursue their own interests. Abel and Cain, Abraham and Lot, Isaac and Ishmael, Jacob and Esau.

History records that it is the minority of people who truly pursue Christ above everything else in their lives.

There are many who go to church. There are many more who would consider themselves to be "believers." But the real test of discipleship is found in the words of the Master Himself.

"Anyone who loves his father or mother more than me is not worthy of me; anyone who loves his son or daughter more than me is not worthy of me."[1]

The qualification for discipleship is clear. There are no educational requirements. There are no ethnic or racial barriers. There are no monetary qualifications, nor are there any background checks.

God's first and only pre-requisite for the would-be disciple is this:

"DO YOU LOVE ME?"

Our relationship with Him must be pre-eminent, placed above our relationship with anyone else, including ourselves, if we are to truly live in Him.

To pursue God means more than going to church. To pursue God means to seek out and discover who He is, and what He is doing in your world, and to press into it with all your heart. It is to love the Lord with all of your heart, soul, mind and strength — which will always result in loving others as you love yourself.

TO PURSUE GOD MEANS TO LOVE CHRIST PASSIONATELY — with all of our hearts.

It is to feel our faith. It is to sustain a flame of godly fervor and not let the fire go out.

Take an ice cube out of the refrigerator, and in a few minutes it becomes a puddle. Take a boiling cup of coffee off the stove, and in a few minutes it is a tepid cup of brown water.

The natural course of life is toward lukewarmness. Yet God is offended by neutrality and to remain passionate about our pursuit of God requires a commitment to constant watchcare over the flame of our hearts.

Let's ask ourselves a piercing question: Just what are we passionate about?

TO PURSUE GOD MEANS TO LOVE CHRIST PERSONALLY — with all of our souls.

Our calling to pursue fellowship with the Lord is not merely a corporate one. It is wonderful to gather with the church and worship the Lord in the fullness of the fellowship. But when we stand, as we all will, before the Father, we will stand alone. It is then that the quality of our fellowship will be truly revealed.

TO PURSUE GOD MEANS TO LOVE CHRIST INTELLIGENTLY — with all of our minds.

But so many believers have allowed their minds to become an indiscriminate dumping ground for all of the world's pollution. Geraldo, Oprah and Phil have desensitized our sense of morality and normalcy. Robocop and Rambo have made bloodshed meaningless. MTV and HBO have robbed a whole generation of our children of their innocence.

To pursue God intelligently means that we choose to live with limitations as to what we allow our minds to dwell upon. It means that we:

"Study to shew thyself approved unto God, a workman that needeth not to be ashamed, rightly dividing the word of truth." (KJV)[2]

TO PURSUE GOD MEANS TO LOVE CHRIST FORCEFULLY — with all of our strength. Thank God for the generations of believers who went before us laboring in His power for the sake of the kingdom of God. Their pursuit of God was not limited to a fifteen minute homily once a week and a five minute devotion once a day. Before the days of electricity and automobiles, the Wesleys crossed a dangerous ocean to preach Christ from town to town. The Spurgeons and Moodys of former years would have shamed most pastors, given today's comfortable expectations. Paul spoke of times when:

"We were under great pressure, far beyond our ability to endure, so that we despaired even of life. Indeed, in our hearts we felt the sentence of death."[3]

But because of Paul's efforts to pursue God forcefully, we have become inheritors with Christ of the promises of God! There is more to us than meets the eye. What strength we can have when we learn that we can:

"...do all things through Christ which strengtheneth me."[4] *(KJV)*

TO PURSUE GOD MEANS TO LOVE CHRIST AUTHENTICALLY
— by loving others as we love ourselves.

Ultimately our love for the Father is proven by the love we show for one another. The authentic outcome of pursuing God is that we will sense His love for the nations and be empowered by His Spirit to go in His Name.

He doesn't ask "Are you intrigued by me?"

He doesn't ask "Are you interested in me?"

He doesn't ask "Do you concur with my commands?"

He doesn't ask "Do you attend my meetings?"

His one penetrating question is the same one He asked Peter three times after his midnight denials — "Do you love me?"

Our answer will show either passing interest or heartfelt passion. And it is the passionate saint who is the true disciple of Christ. Unless we would surrender to His will and purpose, our love is anemic and artificial. Either He is Lord of all or He isn't Lord at all.

THIS IS WHAT IT MEANS TO PURSUE GOD.

A Church of the Nations is a church that places no value on looking the part. It is not attempting to achieve any status except to serve one another out of reverence for Christ. It is building no kingdoms but the kingdom of God, serving no interests but the interests of Christ. Its members are unashamedly, unhesitatingly His disciples in hot pursuit of His will and His ways; individually and corporately.

This is the mission of a Church of the Nations and her members. They are imperfect and still very much under construction. They are in need of much correction and frequent instruction. But they know the goal and seek to keep it ever before them:

To Pursue God — Keeping Him ever in their sights!

To Pursue God — Seeking always to know His will!

To Pursue God — Worshipping Him in spirit and in truth!

This is their quest and the source of their strength and inspiration. When we are still and know that He is God, then we will see that He is exalted among the nations and exalted in the earth!

ENDNOTES

1   Matthew 10:37 "Anyone who loves his father or mother more than me is not worthy of me; anyone who loves his son or daughter more than me is not worthy of me."

2   2 Timothy 2:15 "Study to shew thyself approved unto God, a workman that needeth not to be ashamed, rightly dividing the word of truth."

3   23 Corinthians 1:18-9a "We were under great pressure, far beyond our ability to endure, so that we despaired even of life. Indeed, in our hearts we felt the sentence of death."

4   Philippians 4:13 "...do all things through Christ which strengtheneth me."

5

Advancing the Kingdom

•••

The kingdom advances whenever a person, whoever or wherever they are, steps from darkness to light, from death to life.

What is the kingdom of God? In it's simplest sense the kingdom of God is the place where the King, Jesus, reigns. And where does Christ reign in authority? In the heart of every person who turns to Him in humble repentance and yields to Him as Lord and Savior. Jesus Himself declared: *"The kingdom of God is within you."*[1] Obviously where Christ reigns over a human heart there will be evident change in the external world.[2] People under the true lordship of Jesus Christ will change the institutions and people they come into contact with because the kingdom of God is within them. His Lordship over their hearts and minds will lead them to combat evil and promote righteousness and the external world which is influenced and touched by those under Christ's command will be dramatically impacted for good.[3]

But we should never confuse the external evidence with the inward reality. It is possible to vote for moral legislation, be pro-life, have a conservative political agenda and still be lost from the kingdom of God.

Those under the authority of God's kingdom may be moral, but morality alone is not the same as being a new creature in Christ. New creaturehood comes through a supernatural act of God.[4] It's in response to the individual who comes in humble contrition to the knowledge of their own broken relationship with the Father and their own need to be born of the Spirit, forgiven and delivered[5].

It is in this sense then, regarding the individual, that we speak of advancing the kingdom of God. The kingdom of God is not advanced through political agendas. Such action may be the *result* of the kingdom's advance. The kingdom of God is advanced one heart at a time.

THE PRICELESS VALUE OF ONE

Every single individual in the world is of extraordinary value in the eyes of God. One person responding to the invitation to be reconciled to God solicits the rejoicing of the angels in heaven.[6] The kingdom advances whenever a person, whoever or wherever they are, steps from darkness to light, from death to life.[7] It is said the Jesus did not come to make bad men good. Jesus came to make dead men live![8] Nothing could come closer to the reality than this thought.

The mission of the Church is to advance the kingdom, one human heart at a time, until every nation, tribe, kindred and tongue are represented at the wedding supper of the Lamb. This call to advance the kingdom should always be on our hearts. A Church of the Nations is in constant vigilance for the souls of men, women and children knowing that *"He who wins souls is wise[9]"* and that in eternity those who lead many to repentance shall *"shine — like the stars forever and ever[10]"*.

THE HIDDEN KINGDOM

Unlike every other kingdom that has ever arisen in human history the kingdom of God has no territorial ambitions. We seek no temporal throne of power. We carry no carnal weapons of might and we amass no stockpiles of wealth or glory. Our only territorial ambition is the next human heart.[11] Our only throne, to be seated with Christ in heavenly places.[12] Our weapons are prayer, the Word of God, Faith and the Blood of the Lamb. Our wealth, the riches of Christ. Our hope of glory, Christ in us!

Because of this we cannot be bought by temporal acquisitions of influence. Nor do we rest on our past achievements. As long as someone is still without Christ we have yet to advance the kingdom to it's final borders. All of this sense of mission issues out of a heart that beats with the Father's heart.

Because we've pursued God through prayer, the Word, our worship and fellowship with one another, we've found his heart and been touched by His love for the nations. Always we remember that the nations are defined by God as groupings of people, groupings of people made up of individuals, individuals for whom Christ died and who are loved equally by the Father heart of God.

WIDENING OUR SCOPE

Our compassion and prioritization of the individual, however, should be expressed with a strategic look at the global advancement of the kingdom of God. We must continue our calls for reconciliation among those of our own nation that have been reached with the gospel but have not yet responded to God's invitation. But it is imperative that we balance that concern with the knowledge that there are millions alive today who have never even heard the Name of Jesus Christ. The knowledge of a loving, benevolent Father who sent His only Son into the world as a perfect sacrifice for sin is good news— unknown to them.

"How, then, can they call on the one they have not believed in? And how can they believe in the one of whom they have not heard? And how can they hear without someone preaching to them?"[13]

CHURCH WITH A MISSION

Historically, it seems the advancement of the kingdom globally has been seen as the job of the missions agency or parachurch organization. The local church has viewed this task as peripheral to her own interests and although in some cases there has been a missions department or perhaps a week long missions emphasis in the church calendar, the word "missions" itself seems to elicit yawns from the majority of church members. I dislike the word "missions." It implies a kind of junior-level emphasis that boils down to a number of programs or once-a-year events. I prefer the singular word "Mission."

A Church of the Nations is not a "missions church" implying a limited emphasis on funding, training and sending missionaries to foreign fields. A Church of the Nations is a "Church with a Mission" that recognizes that the advancement of the kingdom — locally, regionally and globally — is the one mission of the Church. It is a church that not only accepts such an ideal with lip service, but one which strategically plans the use of her time, talent and resources to the achievement of that objective. This sense of mission sustains and focuses the local church towards the reaching of the lost locally and globally. The members of a Church of the Nations see themselves as ambassadors of reconciliation:

"We are therefore Christ's ambassadors, as though God were making his appeal through us. We implore you on Christ's behalf: Be reconciled to God."[14]

BLESSED TO BE A BLESSING

A Church of the Nations constantly calls her people to remember that the final sign before the return of Christ to the earth is the global proclamation of the kingdom of God.[15]

As obvious as it sounds, we must remember that we were not blessed with the good news of salvation simply to be blessed. We were blessed to be a blessing.[16] God's promise to Abraham was not only that he would be blessed, but that through him all the nations of the earth would be blessed.[17] Not some of the nations. Not the nations of the West alone. Not the prosperous nations exclusively. But all of the nations of the earth! This is God's promise to Abraham and God is a covenant-keeping God. This is why Peter's first sermon on the day of Pentecost was to:

"—God-fearing Jews from every nation under heaven.[18]*"*

because God's heart has always been for the nations. God sent His Son as the substitute for Man allowing Him to bear the sins of the whole world.[19] God raised him from the dead and lifted him back to His throne in heaven.[20] He filled His Church with the Holy Spirit[21] and called them to the "Mission."[22] His first act through the Church was to give Peter His anointing to preach the good news to men from every nation under heaven and to reawaken his challenge to the people of God. He called them to come to Christ — and then go to the lost world.

THE SUPREME TASK

This mandate, and the Father's heart, remain unchanged. God's heart is for the nations. Can His Church's heart be any different?

"Ask of me, and I will make the nations your inheritance, the ends of the earth your possession."[23]

It is the central belief of a Church of the Nations that God's promises are not vain or empty. A Church of the Nations believes that they can ask of God and He will give a nation as an inheritance.[24]

Seeking, interceding and cooperating with the Father; a Church of the Nations believes that they can fill a seat at the wedding supper of the Lamb[25] with a nation's representatives that are as yet unrepresented. A Church of the Nations will strategically plan to partner with the Father, and others of like mind and heart, to reach the unreached nations as they continue to preach Christ to their own people. They will seek in everyway to advance the kingdom of God in the hearts of men.

We cannot rest in the bosom of salvation content in the knowledge that we possess eternal life while forgetting a lost world. To enter into God's rest is to cease from our own labors and strivings to earn God's favor.[26] It is to rest in the finished work of Christ.

But to enter into His rest is also to enter into His labors.[27] It is to allow His workings to operate through us. This is the rest of God. We enter into it when we cease striving to earn His approval (Because it is already ours through Christ), and we yield our lives to Him as instruments through which He can accomplish His purpose. And what is His purpose?

"And they sang a new song: "You are worthy to take the scroll and to open its seals, because you were slain, and with your blood you purchased men for God from every tribe and language and people and nation."[28]

Reaching the nations, at home and abroad, is the purpose of God.

ENDNOTES

1 Luke 17:21 "nor will people say, 'Here it is,' or 'There it is,' because the kingdom of God is within you."

2 1 John 3:7 Dear children, do not let anyone lead you astray. He who does what is right is righteous, just as he is righteous.

3 1 John 3:3 "Everyone who has this hope in him purifies himself, just as he is pure."

4 2 Corinthians 5:17 "Therefore, if anyone is in Christ, he is a new creation; the old has gone, the new has come!"

5 1 Peter 5:5b All of you, clothe yourselves with humility toward one another, because, "God opposes the proud but gives grace to the humble."

6 Luke 15:10 "In the same way, I tell you, there is rejoicing in the presence of the angels of God over one sinner who repents."

7 Acts 26:18 "—to open their eyes and turn them from darkness to light, and from the power of Satan to God, so that they may receive forgiveness of sins and a place among those who are sanctified by faith in me."

8 John 5:25 "I tell you the truth, a time is coming and has now come when the dead will hear the voice of the Son of God and those who hear will live."

9 Proverbs 11:30 "The fruit of the righteous is a tree of life, and he who wins souls is wise."

10 Daniel 12:3 "Those who are wise will shine like the brightness of the heavens, and those who lead many to righteousness, like the stars for ever and ever."

11 Ephesians 3:17a "—so that Christ may dwell in your hearts through faith."

12 Ephesians 2:6

13 Romans 10:14 "How, then, can they call on the one they have not believed in? And how can they believe in the one of whom they have not heard? And how can they hear without someone preaching to them?"

14 2 Corinthians 5:20b "We are therefore Christ's ambassodors, as though God were making his appeal through us. We implore you on Christ's behalf: Be reconciled to God."

15 Matthew 24:14 "And this gospel of the kingdom will be preached in the whole world as a testimony to all nations, and then the end will come."

16 Genesis 12:2 "I will make you into a great nation and I will bless you; I will make your name great, and you will be a blessing.

17 Genesis 12:3b "— and all peoples on earth will be blessed through you."

18 Acts 2:5b

19 1 John 2:2 "He is the atoning sacrifice for our sins, and not only for ours but also for the sins of the whole world."

20 Ephesians 1:19b-20 "—That power is like the working of his mighty strength, which he exerted in Christ when he raised him from the dead and seated him at his right hand in the heavenly realms,—"

21 Acts 2:4a "—All of them were filled with the Holy Spirit—"

22 Acts 1:8 "But you will receive power when the Holy Spirit comes on you; and you will be my witnesses in Jerusalem, and in all Judea and Samaria, and to the ends of the earth."

23 Psalm 2:8 "Ask for me, and I will make the nations your inheritance, the ends of the earth your possesion."

24 See Appendix -A- "Adopting a Unreached People"

25 Revelation 19:9a "Then the angel said to me, "Write: ` Blessed are those who are invited to the wedding supper of the Lamb!'"

26 Hebrews 4:10 "— for anyone who enters God's rest also rests from his own work —"

27 1 Corinthians 15:58b "— Let nothing move you. Always give yourselves fully to the work of the Lord, because you know that your labor in the Lord is not in vain."

Colossians 1:29 " To this end I labor, struggling with all his energy, which so powerfully works in me."

28 Revelation 5:9 And they sang a new song: You are worthy to take the Scroll and to open its seals, because you were slain, and with your blood you purchased men for God from every tribe and language and people and nation."

CHAPTER

6

Building the Church
•••

When we speak of building the Church, we are not speaking of bricks and mortar. The Church is made of living stones — the saints themselves.

Every building has three primary characteristics. First, the purpose, which is the original reason for construction. Second is the building material which determines the quality of the construction and the length of time the building can be expected to last. Third is the foundation, upon which the whole structure can be safely erected.

The same three characteristics help define the Church. The Apostle Paul spoke of the one foundation that alone can be laid beneath every believer's life. That foundation is Christ himself.[1] It is upon the rock of Jesus that the Church is to be built,[2] and it is hearing and obeying His Word that guarantees a foundation that can stand up to the storms and raging waves that life can produce.[3]

When we speak of building the Church, we are not speaking of bricks and mortar. The Church is made of living stones[4] — the saints themselves.

To build the Church is to lay this firm foundation beneath the life of each believer.

It is to constantly test to see that it is rock — and not sand — that men are building their lives upon.

It is to challenge and dig beneath their external images to uncover the true nature of the basis upon which their faith rests.

If the life of the believer rests upon anything other than Christ, that life will crumble.

As one great hymn puts it,

"My hope is built on nothing less, than Jesus' blood and righteousness. I dare not trust the sweetest frame, but wholly lean on Jesus' Name. On Christ the solid rock I stand, all other ground is sinking sand. All other ground is sinking sand."[5]

ON CHRIST OUR ROCK

We live in a time when there is a great need for revival. But the revival we need is more than just a taste of new wine. It is a return to biblical foundations and solid theology. Many have forgotten the strong anchors of our faith, and many more are in danger in following deceiving spirits.[6]

But, we are called to worship the Lord in spirit and in truth.[7]

Truth is likened to the rudder and compass of a ship. They give stability and direction.

The Spirit, on the other hand, is like the wind against the sails, providing the sense of power. Truth without the Spirit leaves us floating dead in the water. The Spirit without the Word fills our sails and moves us powerfully — but can crash us on the rocks of deception and send us to the bottom of the sea. We need the power of the Holy Spirit to enable us. We also need the stability of God's Word to under gird us.

To build the Church means to disciple those into whose hearts the kingdom of God has advanced so as to ensure their ability to stand when the storms of life fall.

GROWING IN GRACE

Every person in the world falls into one of the following categories:
- Lost and without Christ[8]
- New Christian[9]
- Maturing Believer[10]
- Disciple[11]
- Maker of Disciples[12]
- Maker of Disciple Makers[13]

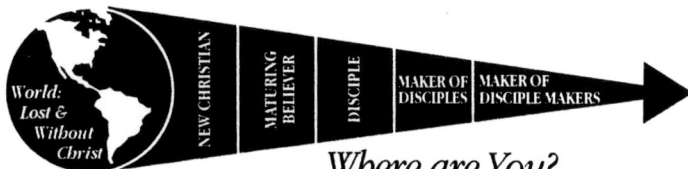

Where are You?

The goal of building the Church is to equip each believer to be able to move down the line from conversion to the place of making disciples. And some will be blessed to see those they have discipled actually making disciples themselves! Every believer is capable of being a part of God's purposes in establishing foundations in the life of another. This is what building the Church is all about.

PASSION OR COMPROMISE?

But upon each Foundation — our acceptance of Jesus — we must also select the materials with which our lives will be constructed. Paul addresses this issue when he divides our choices into two categories. There are gold, silver and costly stones, or wood hay and straw.[14] The test he proposes to influence our decision is the test of fire.[15]

In essence, Paul, speaks to us of the quality of the choices we make each day. Are we investing in things eternal, or are we selling our birthright for a mess of pottage that will be quickly consumed by God's discerning fire?[16]

How often I've stood at the bedside of people who have thrown their entire lives into the amassing of temporal position, power or influence only to find themselves facing death with little of eternity in their portfolio. Or others who have spent their lives in the chains of depression or bitterness, unwilling to release the pain of the past and press into God's divine purposes for their lives.

I am a relatively young man but I have lived for years with a strong sense of my own mortality. It amazes me how many people are living as though they will never die. Some are only a few short years away from eternity, and yet they are squandering their precious remaining days on meaningless temporal pursuits.

Gold, silver or costly stones are things like passion for Jesus, a burden for the lost, a teachable spirit and an obedient heart.

Wood, hay and straw are a passion for playing, a lust for the world, a stubborn spirit and a compromising heart. All of these things will be tested by fire, and only what stands up to the flame will pass through the portals of eternity.

No wonder the psalmist cried to the Lord:

Teach us to number our days aright, that we may gain a heart of wisdom.[17]

A SENSE OF DESTINY

To build our lives with eternal material is the result of living deliberately.

Contemplating our own mortality can contribute to living deliberately. To live deliberately is to plan our own eulogy. It is to determine, under the Holy Sprit's leadership, what His plan and design is for our lives and to hold, unswervingly, to His purpose. It is to die to our small plans that we might live unto His mighty plans. It is to live in the perpetual awareness that each day is a gift and that time cannot be stored away.

Each moment will be either be invested in the eternal or wasted on the temporal.

Are we to be so "heavenly minded" that we are no "earthly good?" No! To the contrary, this is not a call to sour-faced asceticism. Rather, it is a passionate commitment to pressing beyond the shallow and empty promises of the flesh, to find and enjoy the lasting, deeply fulfilling realities of the spirit. It is to:

"—press on toward the goal to win the prize for which God has called me heavenward in Christ Jesus." [18]

that I may:

"—take hold of that for which Christ Jesus took hold of me." [19]

UNITED FOR CAUSE

This leads to the last characteristic of any building: its intended purpose. As we lay the foundations beneath the lives of believers, we must teach them to live for and build upon the foundation of Christ, with a mind toward eternity.

But we must also teach them to ask, "What is the ultimate purpose for this building?"

"In whom all the building fitly framed together groweth unto an holy temple in the Lord: In whom ye also are builded together for an habitation of God through the Spirit." [20]

As the Holy Spirit unites us in our diversity, and indwells us by His presence, we become a habitation for His Life. As we allow His life to be expressed through us, we become a light to a lost world. [21]

As we Pursue God, we come to know His heart.

As we Advance the Kingdom, we come to share His Mission, and prepare for His glorious return!

And as we Build the Church, we strengthen and beautify His bride.

What a high and holy calling belongs to a Church of the Nations! God's heart is for the nations, because God's heart is for people—all people—everywhere!

ENDNOTES

1 1 Corinthians 3:11 "For no one can lay any foundation other than the one already laid, which is Jesus Christ."

2 Matthew 16:16a & 18b Simon Peter answered, "You are the Christ, the Son of the living God." Jesus replied.... and on this rock I will build my church, and the gates of Hades will not overcome it.

3 Matthew 7:24-25 "Therefore everyone who hears these words of mine and puts them into practice is like a wise man who built his house on the rock. The rain came down, the streams rose, and the winds blew and beat against that house; yet it did not fall, because it had its foundation on the rock.

4 1 Peter 2:5 "— you also, like living stones, are being built into a spiritual house to be a holy priesthood, offering spiritual sacrifices acceptable to God through Jesus Christ."

5 "The Solid Rock". Text: Edward Mote, Music: William B. Bradbury. The Hymnal for Worship and Celebration; Word Music, Waco, Texas; page 404

6 1 Timothy 4:1 "The Spirit clearly says that in later times some will abandon the faith and follow deceiving spirits and things taught by demons."

7 John 4:23 "Yet a time is coming and has now come when the true worshipers will worship the Father in spirit and truth, for they are the kind of worshipers the Father seeks."

8 Ephesians 2:12 "remember that at that time you were separate from Christ, excluded from citizenship in Israel and foreigners to the covenants of the promise, without hope and without God in the world."

9 1 Corinthians 3:2 "I gave you milk, not solid food, for you were not yet ready for it. Indeed, you are still not ready."
1 Peter 2:2 "Like newborn babies, crave pure spiritual milk, so that by it you may grow up in your salvation,"

10 1 John 2:14 " I write to you, young men, because you are strong, and the word of God lives in you, and you have overcome the evil one. "

11 Luke 14:26-27;33 "If anyone comes to me and does not hate his father and mother, his wife and children, his brothers and sisters — yes, even his own life — he cannot be my disciple. And anyone who does not carry his cross and follow me cannot be my disciple.
....In the same way, any of you who does not give up everything he has cannot be my disciple."

John 12:25 "The man who loves his life will lose it, while the man who hates his life in this world will keep it for eternal life."

Mark 8:35-37 "For whoever wants to save his life will lose it, but whoever loses his life for me and for the gospel will save it. What good is it for a man to gain the whole world, yet forfeit his soul? Or what can a man give in exchange for his soul?"

Luke 5:11 "So they pulled their boats up on shore, left everything and followed him."

12 Matthew 28:19-20 "Therefore go and make disciples of all nations, baptizing them in the name of the Father and of the Son and of the Holy Spirit, and teaching them to obey everything I have commanded you. And surely I am with you always, to the very end of the age."

1 Timothy 1:1-2 "Paul, an apostle of Christ Jesus by the command of God our Savior and of Christ Jesus our hope, To Timothy my true son in the faith: Grace, mercy and peace from God the Father and Christ Jesus our Lord."

13 2 Timothy 2:1-2 "You then, my son, be strong in the grace that is in Christ Jesus. And the things you have heard me say in the presence of many witnesses entrust to reliable men who will also be qualified to teach others."

14 1 Corinthians 3:12-13 "If any man builds on this foundation using gold, silver, costly stones, wood, hay or straw, his work will be shown for what it is, because the Day will bring it to light. It will be revealed with fire, and the fire will test the quality of each man's work."

15 1 Corinthians 3:14-15 "If what he has built survives, he will receive his reward. If it is burned up, he will suffer loss; he himself will be saved, but only as one escaping through the flames."

16 Genesis 25:34 "Then Jacob gave Esau some bread and some lentil stew. He ate and drank, and then got up and left. So Esau despised his birthright."

17 Psalm 90:12 Teach us to number our days aright, that we may gain a heart of wisdom.

18 Phillipians 3:14 "—press on toward the goal to win the prize for which God has called me heavenward in Christ Jesus."

19 Phillipians 3:12b "—take hold of that for which Christ Jesus took hold of me."

20 Ephesians 2:21-22 (KJV) "In whom all building fitly framed together groweth unto an holy temple in the Lord: In whom ye also are builded together for an habitation of God through the Spirit."

21 Matthew 5:14-16 "You are the light of the world. A city on a hill cannot be hidden. Neither do people light a lamp and put it under a bowl. Instead they put it on its stand, and it gives light to everyone in the house. In the same way, let your light shine before men, that they may see your good deeds and praise your Father in heaven."

CHAPTER

7

Becoming a Servant
•••

"In the person of Christ we see a complete reversal of the corporate triangle."

Within every church there are two active entities. There is the spiritual body of Christ, made up of those who have been born of the Spirit, and are engaged in the actual work of the Lord. And there is the corporation made up of the policies, procedures and red tape that help to govern the affairs of the church.

The spiritual body is characterized by prayer, worship, evangelism, sacraments, love, fellowship and the like. The corporation is characterized by requisitions, purchase orders, budget reports, board of director's minutes, Robert's rules of order, taxes, and insurance papers, mortgage notes and bank statements and the like.

Every church with which I've been affiliated has both systems at work.

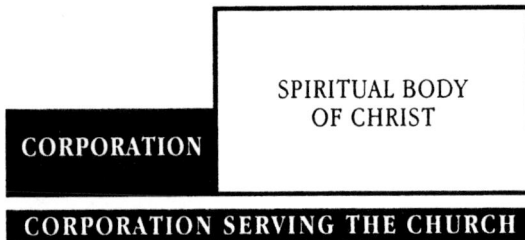

```
                    ┌──────────────────────┐
                    │                      │
                    │    SPIRITUAL BODY     │
                    │      OF CHRIST       │
        ┌───────────┤                      │
        │ CORPORATION│                      │
        └───────────┴──────────────────────┘
    ■■■■■■■■■■■■■■■■■■■■■■■■■■■■■■■■■■■■■■■■■■■■■■
    CORPORATION SERVING THE CHURCH
```

A NOBLE BEGINNING

It all starts like this. A group of believers get together with a vision to start a church. Their dream is to gather saints together to worship, grow in the Word and reach their community for Christ. They are disorganized and inefficient, but they have a heart for Christ and a desire to touch their city. When the devoted few make the commitment, the process is underway.

At some point, in order to secure facilities and pay a pastor; to receive offerings and provide tax credit; the suggestion is made to incorporate and become a legal entity. By-Laws are borrowed or adopted.

This corporate charter may be a page or a page and a half long, perhaps longer. But whatever its size, one thing is guaranteed. It is going to grow. Not slowly or over a great period of time. This corporate system will grow like a weed until it eventually threatens to take over everything and everyone in the church.

What was created to serve the spiritual body of Christ so that they could be about the business of the church now *becomes* the business of the church.

Prayer, worship, evangelism and fellowship give way to board meetings and business reports. We started by taking up offerings to do the work of the ministry. We end up doing the work of the ministry in order to keep the offerings up. We have pastors to pay, buildings to maintain and mortgages to honor. We can't get Bibles to the prison ministry's new converts because we don't have a purchase order.

The corporation was created to serve the spiritual body of Christ. Before long the spiritual body of Christ ends up of serving the corporation.

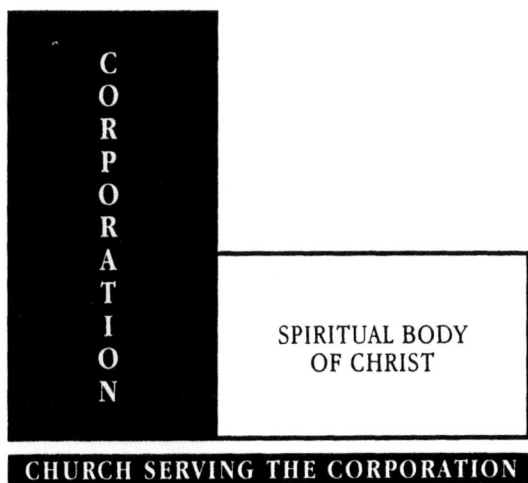

```
C
O
R
P
O
R
A
T
I              SPIRITUAL BODY
O                 OF CHRIST
N
```

CHURCH SERVING THE CORPORATION

As the policies and procedures become more formalized, the spiritual body of Christ takes on more and more of the characteristics of a corporation. This is particularly true in regards to her leadership structure.

Every corporation has a corporate ladder to climb. At the top of the ladder is the CEO (Better known as the Senior Pastor). Below him are the elders, followed by the pastoral staff or deacons (in some cases, reversed). Then come workers in the church and volunteers.

LAST OF ALL IS THE CONGREGATION.

Because a corporation is controlled by those with the highest positions, the activity within a corporation becomes simple. The race is to get to the top.

Obviously not everyone can be the Senior Pastor. There are also limitations of gifting and calling to obtain an associate pastoral position.

But there can be "confidants" to those in high position. Each elder has his group of "close friends" who are "in the loop."

All of this is natural, I suppose. A part of human nature. But in the corporate church the intrigue and ladder climbing become the game itself. A heart for the lost is exchanged for an eye for the bigger office or more influential position.

None of this is talked about, of course. Many playing the game are not really conscious of the changes taking place in the authenticity of their faith.

Soon a well-oiled machine is operating with each person playing their part. The performers are on the stage being admired and honored. The supporting players are given their due respect. Those closest to the positions of influence have the best seats in the house.

And out there, in the pew, sits the audience.

They are supposed to:

suit up

show up

pay up and

shut up.

Their role is to observe. God forbid they should try to participate, except appropriately, as needed (rarely). They would simply get in the way of the action.

Their gifts and callings are irrelevant to the corporation. All that is needed is their attention and their resources. Everything else is covered.

To be fair, it's not a bad deal for the audience either. They arrive on time, find a seat, are moved and inspired, pay their offering and leave — knowing that no one really expects them to experience any sort of radical change that would demand anything uncomfortable.

This corporate clergy-laity gap creates a church of spectators and a pastorate of superstars. Like a basketball game in the coliseum, there are a handful of very gifted people on the court, and a whole lot of other people sitting around and watching.

GETTING RIGHT SIDE UP

But when Christ envisioned the Church, He saw something much different. This is evident from His actions at the last supper when he wrapped Himself with a towel, poured a basin of water and washed His

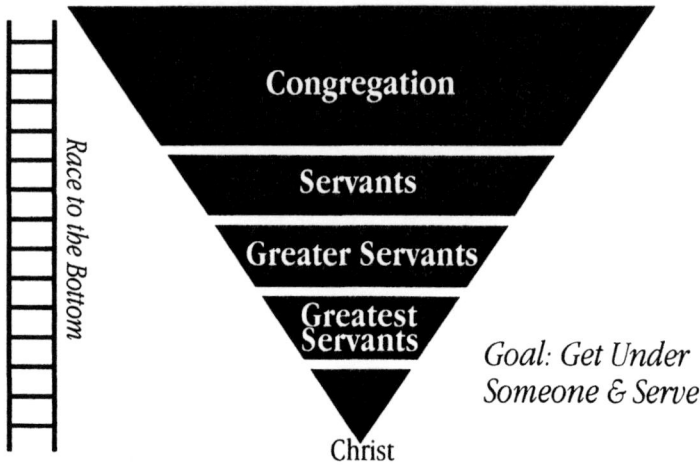

Race to the Bottom

Congregation

Servants

Greater Servants

Greatest Servants

Christ

Goal: Get Under Someone & Serve

SPIRITUAL BODY OF CHRIST

disciples' feet (very un-CEO like). His words at that moment were the Magna Charta of the Church's calling:

"You call me 'Teacher' and 'Lord,' and rightly so, for that is what I am.

Now that I, your Lord and Teacher, have washed your feet, you also should wash one another's feet. I have set you an example that you should do as I have done for you.

I tell you the truth, no servant is greater than his master, nor is a messenger greater than the one who sent him. Now that you know these things, you will be blessed if you do them."[1]

Elsewhere Christ taught His disciples:

"—whoever wants to become great among you must be your servant, and whoever wants to be first must be your slave — just as the Son of Man did not come to be served, but to serve, and to give his life as a ransom for many."[2]

In the person of Christ we see a complete reversal of the corporate triangle. In the Church, the race is to the bottom of the spiritual body of Christ. It is to get under someone and serve them.

This is the example Christ left when He encountered people: When He met Nicodemus, he served as a guide.[3] When He met the ten lepers, He served as a healer.[4] When he met the woman caught in adultery, He served as a forgiver.[5] When He met the thief on the cross, He served as a redeemer.[6] On Golgotha, He served as the Savior and Sin-bearer as He bore its weight and punishment for the whole world.[7] And even now, seated in the heavens, He serves as intercessor[8] and advocate![9]

No wonder Paul wrote the Philippians to:

"Let this mind be in you, which was also in Christ Jesus: Who, being in the form of God, thought it not robbery to be equal with God: But made himself of no reputation, and took upon him the form of a servant, and was made in the likeness of men:"[10] (KJV)

The leadership of the Church operates in their calling when they exist to find, teach, train and release the giftings and callings of the congregation. The congregation in turn can do the work of the ministry.[11]

There are no stars in the Church but the "Bright and morning star",[12] Jesus Himself. He is the Head of the Church[13] and her Chief Shepherd.[14] All of the rest of us who have the privilege of pastoring are merely His undershepherds[15] entrusted with the task of awakening and calling forth the giftings of others.

The job of the Church is too important, and too large, to be left to a handful of people. The whole Church must respond to the call of the Father, if the nations are to be reached.

A Church of the Nations is a church that serves. They serve the Lord first, through worship and prayer. They serve one another secondly, through discipleship and equipping as they minister to one another in love. They serve the world always, as ambassadors of reconciliation committed to the task of "going" in the Name of Jesus.

A Church of the Nations is a church of servants. Those who are greatest among us are the greatest servants of all.

ENDNOTES

1 John 13:13-17

2 Mathew 20:26-28

3 John 3:1-21

4 Luke 17:11-19

5 John 8:2-11

6 Luke 23:40-43

7 2 Corinthians 5:21

8 Romans 8:34; Hebrews 7:25

9 1 John 2:1

10 Philippians 2:5-7

11 Ephesians 4:11-12 "It was he who gave some to be apostles, some to be prophets, some to be evangelists, and some to be pastors and teachers, to prepare God's people for works of service, so that the body of Christ may be built up..."

12 Revelation 22:16

13 Colossians 1:18

14 1 Peter 5:4

15 John 21:16

8

*Locally Igniting:
Answering the Questions*
•••

"The Holy Scriptures continue to be the most contemporary writings ever penned."

Bioethics and the origins of man, assisted suicide and gay rights, cyberspace and digital technology, global trade organizations and ethnic cleansing: These and a myriad of other troubling ethical frontiers face the generation that will grow old in the twenty-first century.[1]

From the most basic issues of right and wrong, male and female, morality and immorality to the most ancient conflicts of good versus evil, the future versus the past, and war versus peace, the next generation will be forced to find the answers to a dizzying array of increasingly complex problems. The quiet, unchanging neighborhood of predictable tomorrows is gone forever. The "global village" has arrived.

The changes that communication and interactive technology will bring to our lives can only be imagined. As the need for answers to the hyperspeed world of tomorrow increases, the Church must be making preparations today to be a viable competitor in the market-place of ideas.

In every city and town there will be a deepening need for churches that can truly model the kingdom of God in the midst of the rising and falling kingdoms of men. Increasingly, as the solutions of men prove bankrupt, the church that speaks with integrity and walks with purpose will be surprised to find listening and hungry hearts.[2]

Let's face it. As one pastor puts it, the most segregated hour is America remains Sunday morning at 11:00 a.m. Does the church truly want to show Christ's heart for the nations? Imagine the response to a fellowship that practices (and not just preaches) unity in diversity, servanthood to one another, clear ethical boundaries and the recognition of a divine plan for the ages. Such a church will be a catalyst for great revival in the days ahead.

But a church that clings to the patterns of the past, fantasizing that the world will not change around them, will become, like the empty cathedrals of Europe, a monument to their modern irrelevance.

The Holy Scriptures continue to be the most contemporary writings ever penned[3]. Their precepts and perspectives shatter the empty promises of pop culture and proclaim today the so-called "break-through findings" of tomorrow's headlines.

God's Word is relevant because God's Word is true. Truth is timeless.

The problem with the church, as someone once remarked, is not that it has failed — but that it has never been successfully tried!

A Church of the Nations will grow beyond the pettiness of inner church politics to the larger vision of God's love for the people of the earth. As pews become training ground for ambassadors rather than spectator seats for critics, the backbiting and disunity will diminish. When a Church of the Nations steps out of the protected facilities and begins to take their religion to the streets, schools and office parks, the gates of hell will be forced to fall![4]

DEFINING THE NATIONS

A Church of the Nations is not in competition with the other churches in the city. Their heart is for the lost to come to Christ, the redeemed to be discipled, the discipled to be equipped and the equipped to be sent.

As they look at their city with an eye to the harvest, they begin to discern the "nations" all around them. There is the "nation of children" and the "nation of youth".

SINGLE PARENTS ARE A "NATION," AS IS CORPORATE AMERICA.

From college students and mothers with small children to foreign students or businessmen, each represents a group with a common "culture" and a shared "language" that needs to be strategically penetrated by ambassadors of reconciliation.

As a locally igniting force, a Church of the Nations will support and encourage any ministry that desires to work together to pursue God, advance the kingdom and build the Church. Gaining members is balanced by the desire to send members, out into the community, with the necessary skills to bless others and promote the cause of Christ.

Although the balance between inreach and outreach ministries is challenging to maintain, a Church of the Nations refuses to capitulate to the natural tendency to think of themselves first. It is their conviction that discipleship without mission becomes an exercise in futility and produces ineffective believers who pose no real threat to the kingdom of darkness.

The man and woman in the pew must begin to think in terms of personal involvement in the mission of the church to the world. Only then will the truths taught them become more than theory or unapplied doctrine.

In the marketplace of life, armed and equipped with the Word and the Spirit, faith comes alive as each member enters into their "nation" representing Christ the King.

As long as faith remains silent in our hearts, its potential, like a dormant seed, is unrealized.

But when that seed is removed from the comfort zone of safety and thrust into the soil of a lost world, its dormant life is activated. Its leaves can heal the nations.[5]

To be locally igniting is to take the blazing truths of God's Word into our local community with the conviction that within its page are the answers for a confused world. It is to believe that there are no questions that the world is asking that the Word cannot answer with life-changing wisdom.

On the brink of a confused and frightening twenty-first century, it's comforting to know that the King we bow to has been there before us.

Tomorrow's perplexing problems have already been answered by Him — today.

ENDNOTES

1   Daniel 12:4
    "But you, Daniel, close up and seal the words of the scroll until the time of the end. Many will go here and there to increase knowledge."

    Ecclesiastes 1:18
    "For with much wisdom comes much sorrow; the more knowledge, the more grief."

2   Matthew 13:44-46

"The kingdom of heaven is like treasure hidden in a field. When a man found it, he hid it again, and then in his joy went and sold all he had and bought that field. "Again, the kingdom of heaven is like a merchant looking for fine pearls. When he found one of great value, he went away and sold everything he had and bought it."

3   Matthew 24:35 "Heaven and earth will pass away, but my words will never pass away."

4   Matthew 16:18

5   Revelation 22:1-2

"Then the angel showed me the river of the water of life, as clear as crystal, flowing from the throne of God and of the Lamb down the middle of the great street of the city. On each side of the river stood the tree of life, bearing twelve crops of fruit, yielding its fruit every month. And the leaves of the tree are for the healing of the nations."

Psalm 1:1-3

"Blessed is the man who does not walk in the counsel of the wicked or stand in the way of sinners or sit in the seat of mockers. But his delight is in the law of the LORD, and on his law he meditates day and night. He is like a tree planted by streams of water, which yields its fruit in season and whose leaf does not wither. Whatever he does prospers."

Impacting Regionally:
Releasing the Saints
•••

> *"To be regionally impacting means to promote anything that promotes Christ, regardless of who gets the credit."*

Wherever a Church of the Nations emerges, there are individuals in surrounding communities whose hearts rejoice at the news. Pastors and laymen, seasoned soldiers of Christ and young zealots hear the good news and make the journey to see for themselves.

Inevitably the call to "go" will awaken hearts within the local body as well, as they begin to contemplate the needs in nearby cities where the richness of spiritual challenge is limited or non-existent.

When this begins to happen, how should a pastor respond? It's always painful to watch as those who have come to Christ, been equipped and become mature fellow laborers in the mission move away from the local body into another city or town. The natural tendency of any pastor is to want to keep these precious and zealous warriors on the team as encouragers and burden-bearers in the local work.

But a Church of the Nations exists to equip the saints and to release them into their calling.

When some are called to relocate and carry the Church of the Nations vision into another city, we must rejoice in that calling and bless them in their going. We must see it as evidence of God's hand on our own ministry, as those believers have reached greater maturity.

As they go, may their ministries be fruitful and may the kingdom of God advance boldly! And, as we are able, may we serve them in their going, just as they have served us while they were among us.

This is the heart of a Church of the Nations, as of her Lord.

SERVING THE SAINTS

To be regionally impacting also means that we serve local pastors and churches by including them in our successes even when it doesn't directly benefit us in any way. It means to promote anything that promotes Christ regardless of who gets the credit.

A Church of the Nations will seek to share its skills, resources, successful programs and philosophy with anyone who is seeking a model of ministry.

We cling to no one but Christ; we embrace all who embrace Him.

Where other churches or ministries are having impact, we do not seek to re-create the wheel. We will partner with, or refer people to ministries that can meet needs more effectively.

A Church of the Nations will even draw a map to another church if it is a better fit for an exploring heart! Releasing shepherds, and sheep, into their calling is an integral part of a Church of the Nation's philosophy of ministry.

PARTNERS IN MINISTRY

As each member identifies and seeks to penetrate his or her own local "nation," ministries that regionally impact that same focus group may create opportunities for expanded outreach. A local chapter of Christian motorcyclists can become equippers for a regional conference on street evangelist. A Christian businessman's group can launch a three-city luncheon to inspire other men to start a group in their community. An experienced youth pastor can host a high school outreach, and then sponsor a crusade outside his school system to show other youth pastors how to penetrate public schools.

A Church of the Nations encourages individuals to be sensitive to others of similar calling — even to those who have gone ahead in the same ministry area — and partner with them. We have both a privilege and a responsibility to enter into those works which he has *"prepared in advance for us to do"*.[1]

AWAKENING THE CHURCH

A Church of the Nations never wearies of calling people out into a hurting world and seeking to awaken their gifts and spiritual aptitudes.

As we move out in ministry and gain a deeper understanding of the Father's heart for the nations, our desire to maximize our stewardship of the gospel heightens. Igniting our individual "Jerusalems" leads to a desire to impact our "Judeas and Samarias".[2]

But for the person in pursuit of God, who works actively to advance the kingdom and build the Church, passion will soon develop toward becoming a co-laborer in the ultimate goal: becoming globally influential in the fulfillment of the mission of Christ, even "to the ends of the earth."

To participate locally, regionally and globally in the cause of Christ is a great adventure of faith which brings vitality and vision to a Church of the Nations.

What a harvest has ripened as we peer into the dawn of a new millennium![3] What a tragedy if we miss the opportunity to leave a legacy with an impact...for eternity.

What an honor to co-labor with Christ.

ENDNOTES

1   Ephesians 2:10 "For we are God's workmanship, created in Christ Jesus to do good works, which God prepared in advance for us to do."

2   Acts 1:8a "But you will receive power when the Holy Spirit comes on you; and you will be my witnesses in Jerusalem, and in all Judea and Samaria — "

3   John 4:35 " Do you not say, 'Four months more and then the harvest'? I tell you, open your eyes and look at the fields! They are ripe for harvest. "

*Influencing Globally:
Targeting the Nations*

•••

T he Mission of the Father has never once wavered since His promise was given to Abraham in Genesis chapter twelve.

Through Abraham's seed, Jesus Christ,[1] every people group on earth will one day be blessed.[2] No tribe of man will be excluded from representation and participation in the new heaven and the new earth.

It is not the Father's will that any individual should perish but that all should come to repentance.[3] But it is also not God's will that any nation should perish but that all should have a seat at the wedding supper of the Lamb.

We know that. But do we really believe it? Do we really live it?

A NEW CREATION

The scriptures are unceasing in their proclamation of a coming day of new birth for the heavens and the earth.[4] This new birth will come out of the destruction of the old order of things.[5] Only those who have responded in faith to Christ will be preserved unto that new creation.[6]

It is the Father's will to have representatives from every tribe and nation and kindred and tongue in the kingdom of heaven, which will be eternal and undefiled.

Just as the ark of Noah represented the one refuge from the coming destruction, so Christ is the one refuge from the certain judgment of a Holy God on a rebellious and ruinous world order. And in the same way that God preserved His wonderful diversity and creativity in the sparing of the animals, the Father is determined to preserve the diversity of humanity by the salvation of representatives from every tribe and nation and kindred and tongue.

The value of a single soul from an unreached and unrepresented people is so important to the Father that He would withhold his coming again to see that one turn to Him and find grace. Although it is not the Father's will for any to perish, the sad truth is that many will. They will perish because of their stubborn refusal to respond to the light that God has left us as His witness to the world[7]. They will perish because of the rebellion in their own hearts that drives them to choose sin rather than search for salvation.

But within every tribe and nation there are those who will:

"—hear the voice of the Son of God and those who hear will live."[8]

RECONCILING THE NATIONS

The Father is unrelenting in His heart's pursuit for the nations; His covenant to Abraham to bless all nations through Christ binds Him to fulfill His promise.

Our purchase by the blood of Christ binds us as well. We are bound to be vessels through which His grace can be poured out on a wounded world.[9]

We are the Father's instruments of reconciliation to the world.[10]

Our mandate is clear; our resource is Christ Himself as He goes with us into the nations.[11] This mandate from the Father means that we must, in order to be a New Testament church, plan and execute a strategic cooperation with the body of Christ globally.

We must work with others to target those nations that, to date, have no living witness of Christ among them. This strategic targeting of the nations must be the work of the local church, as well as the mission organization, if the task is to be accomplished.

We cannot continue to preach the gospel to our own nation exclusively while ignoring the hundreds of millions who have had no historical witness of Christ.

Critical to targeting "new" nations is the realization that a strategic aim is needed. There are many nations that we would view as missionary nations that in truth have had access to the gospel for generations. Not that our efforts among these nations should cease or even be scaled back. But at some point we must cry out for those nations who have never heard the gospel the first time.

We must continue to preach Christ to those people groups who have heard the good news in the hope that they will turn to Christ and live. But this concern must be balanced by a commitment to go, let go or help go to those who have never heard.

CATCHING THE VISION

The task of penetrating every unreached people group in the world is so achievable that it could easily be accomplished within a decade if the body of Christ would catch a vision, cooperate and strategically execute a plan of targeting the nations. As a pastor, I am convinced that the local church is the key to the fulfillment of the great commission (defined as targeting and leaving a living witness of the Church among every tribe and nation and kindred and tongue). From the local church can come the resources. From the local church can come the messengers. From the local church can come the prayer covering. From the local church can come the sustained intercession that responds to the Father's invitation to:

"Ask of me, and I will make the nations your inheritance, the ends of the earth your possession".[12]

It is not the pith helmet or machete that are the modern tools of the ambassador's trade. Where indigenous native believers are unavailable, it is the surgeon's scalpel, the engineer's notebook computer, the economists' calculations and the English teacher's conjugations. These are the skills that will open the doors to the limited access nations of the twenty-first century.

The tourist tradesman and the heavy equipment operator will be able to go where the seminarian could never go.

The Mission is no longer for the theologian (It never was!). It is for fishermen, tax collectors and tent makers. It is for men and women, young and old, who have found the Father's heart and become a kingdom of priests for the nations.

THE THIRD WAVE

But the greatest mission force alive today are the tens of thousands of native missionaries who already speak the language and already have the will to go to their own people in culturally relevant ways. This is the third wave of world missions (after the apostolic and colonial years), with which the church in the West must cooperate if we are to participate in the Father's purposes in our generation.

By linking our resources to their needs, we can enable this great sea of evangelists to win whole people groups for Christ!

What a crown for a local congregation of believers to lay at the Savior's feet! A nation, seated at the wedding supper of the lamb, because a local church dared to believe God's Word and partner with Him. A local church that dared to become, as the Church was destined to be, a Church of the Nations!

ENDNOTES

1 Galatians 3:16 The promises were spoken to Abraham and to his seed. The Scripture does not say "and to seeds," meaning many people, but "and to your seed," meaning one person, who is Christ.

2 Galatians 3:8 The Scripture foresaw that God would justify the Gentiles by faith, and announced the gospel in advance to Abraham: "All nations will be blessed through you."

3 2 Peter 3:9 " The Lord is not slow in keeping his promise, as some understand slowness. He is patient with you, not wanting anyone to perish, but everyone to come to repentance."

4 Revelation 21:1 "Then I saw a new heaven and a new earth, for the first heaven and the first earth had passed away, and there was no longer any sea."

5 2 Peter 3:7b;10b "...the present heavens and earth are reserved for fire, being kept for the day of judgment and destruction of ungodly men...The heavens will disappear with a roar; the elements will be destroyed by fire, and the earth and everything in it will be laid bare."

6 John 14:6 Jesus answered, "I am the way and the truth and the life. No one comes to the Father except through me.

7 Romans 1:19b-20 "—what may be known about God is plain to them, because God has made it plain to them. For since the creation of the world God's invisible qualities — his eternal power and divine nature — have been clearly seen, being understood from what has been made, so that men are without excuse. "

   2 Peter 3:5 "But they deliberately forget that long ago by God's word the heavens existed and the earth was formed out of water and by water. "

8 John 5:25 "—hear the voice of the Son of God and those who hear will live."

9 1 Corinthians 6:19b-20 "—You are not your own; you were bought at a price. Therefore honor God with your body."

10 2 Corinthians 5:18-20

11 Matthew 28:20 "— And surely I am with you always, to the very end of the age."

12 Psalm 2:8 "Ask of me, and I will make the nations your inheritance, the ends of the earth your possession".

Equipping the Saints

•••

"The theory of ministry and the practice of ministry need to be married again."

Perhaps you've heard the story of the young man who wanted to learn to play the piano. At his first lesson the instructor pointed out a seat for the student and then took the piano bench for himself. After forty minutes of extraordinary playing, by the teacher, he abruptly arose and announced that the first lesson was over.

After three months repeating the same scenario, the student's first recital was scheduled. When the student failed miserably the teacher looked at the young man's father and said "What a shame. All that time and money and he didn't learn a thing!"

Sometimes it seems that the Church's approach to discipleship is similar. We come to church. We take a seat. We learn about the Great Commission, we sing about God's heart for the nations, we talk about the Father's plan for the ages. But then the lesson is over — and we never get our hands on the piano and play!

I have traveled extensively, for many years, working with agencies on foreign fields teaching and being involved in short-term evangelism opportunities. I have always been amazed at the ability of organizations like Youth with a Mission or Operation Mobilization to take a typical non-descript man or woman in the pew and unlock their gifts and abilities. People who the local church had written off long ago as "non-leadership material" are witnessing today on the streets of cities that range from Hong Kong to Rome, Budapest to Burbank. All because their hidden potential was released.

THE MEASURE OF A LEADER

In the Church today we tend to determine leadership by the ability to acquire and retain knowledge. The more a person knows, the more they are viewed as superior.

We don't much notice whether they ever pray. As long as they can teach about prayer and bring out the Greek or Hebrew, we're impressed.

It doesn't matter if he cares for the poor, as long as he can move us to feel like we should.

And the Great Commission? How many people are experts on the need who have never operated in the ministry!

The reason so many saints are uninterested in the mission of Christ is because we've convinced them that they really can't be trusted to do it. We have reinforced, visually, secretly, directly and indirectly that there really are only a handful of people who qualify to be ambassadors of reconciliation.

You either have it or you don't. And if you don't, just find a pew and be thankful for salvation and the promise of heaven. Stay out of the way and let the experts do the job.

The road into ministry for most people is so extensive and so disqualifying that they would sooner become a neurosurgeon than be equipped and released into meaningful ministry! We have removed the acquisition of knowledge so far from active participation in ministry that the motivation to learn is becoming virtually non-existent.

A DIFFERENT MODEL

But I have seen a different model. Not in the local church, but on the mission field.

I'll never forget being in a room in Amsterdam filled to capacity with people worshipping reverently. I had never experienced such an intensity of worship in my life, though I had been in churches where thousands of worshippers gathered weekly.

What was the difference? Within minutes, these same worshippers would be dividing into teams to go out into the streets of Amsterdam to minister one-on-one with prostitutes and drug addicts, college students and businessmen. Their depth of worship was birthed out of their desperate need for His strength, love and courage.

It wasn't worship for worship's sake, you see. It was worship that flowed out of a sense of mission and urgent need.

I have taught in schools in Hamburg, Germany and found famished hearts who, after three hours of lecture were crying out for even more insight.

Why the hunger? Not because of my teaching, I assure you —

these same truths had been expressed to others without this result. Rather, it was because on Monday of the next week they were leaving the comfort of the classroom and embarking to cities in North Africa and Eastern Russia to take answers from the Word to a confused and darkened world.

Their hunger was birthed out of that same sense of mission and urgent need.

The saints must stop asking the question," How good was the sermon" and start asking the question, "How clear is my path of response?" We must stop looking at and admiring the menu and start enjoying the meal!

It is time, past time, for the saints to stop worshipping to worship and stop learning to learn. It is time for the people of God to be equipped and released to do the work of the ministry.

The theory of ministry and the practice of ministry need to be married again. And a Church of the Nations is, without apology, committed to a ministry for every member.

APPRENTICESHIP INTO MINISTRY

A crucial key to equipping the saints is developing a discipleship ministry that doesn't just result in acquiring knowledge. We need a discipleship ministry that focuses on acquiring skills and useable competencies.

As important and cardinal as theology and doctrine are in discipleship, effective ambassadors need enhanced abilities in communication, leading small groups, time management, goal setting and personality traits. They need to become familiar with their spiritual gifts and learn to assess their strengths and weaknesses in light of a particular interface with a ministry of opportunity. They need help in prioritization of values and recognition of their unique potential to contribute to reaching a focused "nation" whether home or abroad.

They need a "yellow brick road" from ministry-vision, through the acquisition of ministry-skill, to the release into ministry-practice.

This is true discipleship.

More important than anything, they need to know how significant they are to the Mission. They are key to the success or failure of the goal. They are the ambassadors of reconciliation to a world alienated from God. Each believer is indispensable if the purposes of the Father are to be realized among the nations.

NO ONE IS CALLED TO DO NOTHING.

The philosophy of ministry of a Church of the Nations isn't to equip the saints to simply become "Knowers of the Word." It is to train the saints to become "Doers of the Word."

As participation is given high priority, the worship, fellowship and learning of the people will escalate into new levels of expression.

The Church of the Lord Jesus Christ must awaken from its sleep and receive the light of Christ. Each member, (that includes you!) must have before them a clear pathway into ministry.

A Church of the Nations serves every member's calling and works to release them into the world.

May we all work while it is yet day, because:

"—Night is coming, when no one can work." [1]

ENDNOTES

1   John 9:4

12

Focusing on the Family

•••

"Punishment is corrective. But calling a family to invest their lives in an eternal kingdom is preventive."

"What does it profit a man if he gains the whole world and loses his soul?"[1] The question could be further asked, "What does a man profit if he wins the nations, but loses his family?"

The first and most important "nation" that any of us are called to win and disciple is the nation of our own family.[2] Our ministry out to the world is only effective to the extent that our ministry into our family is authentic.

If we are in disunity as husbands and wives or have lost the respect of our children, then our testimony to the nations will ring hollow.[3] It is critical to the success of a Church of the Nations that it is built upon strong and devoted families made up of fathers who spiritually lead their households, mothers who pray and children who obey their parents.

If we can't rule our homes with love and authority, we can't be effective leaders in the church.[4]

THE EXAMPLE OF ISRAEL

The first institution that God ordained was not the Church. It wasn't even the nation of Israel or the temple. The first institution initiated by God was marriage;[5] the soil of the family.

God set up Israel with a priesthood, but through the Sabbath meal, he established the Father as the priest over his household.[6]

The most important moment in any young boy's life was the day of his bar mitzvah. A bar mitzvah is the moment when a son became a "son of the law" (*bar* - son of; *mitzvah* - the law or commandment) and he was able to read from the Torah and participate with the men in the worship of God.

Male infants were circumcised on the eighth day of their life as a sign of the covenant relationship with God into which they had been born.[7] All of this was done under the authority of the mother and father and the family was to be the place of primary instruction in the history and beliefs of the faith.[8]

The Passover meal was symbolically important in one regard

particularly; *there was only one lamb slain per household.[9]* As the head of the household walked in obedience to take the blood of the lamb and apply it to the door posts of his home, he was able to procure God's protection for all of those within the house.[10]

Throughout the early history and culture of Israel, every child was being prepared to be a part of a covenant community with a unique calling on their lives. They saw themselves as the people of God called to be light to the nations.[11]

A TRAGIC COMPROMISE

But after the battles had been won and the enemies subdued, the families of Israel became lazy in their instruction and compromising in their attitudes toward a lost world.[12] Their children began to inter-marry with the idolatrous nations around them and their hearts were drawn away into the same idolatry.

Because they began to lose their distinctive calling to be a kingdom of priests to the nations, they began to seek blessing and pleasure for their own sake.

This decline in the family and the sanctuary of the home led the sons and daughters of idolatrous Israel to be taken away into captivity and slavery.[13]

When the families were lost the nation was lost as well. It was because the children of Israel saw a spiritual void in their homes that they began to explore the gods of the nations around them. Their fall into idolatry came as a result of the spiritual lethargy they saw in their parents towards the purposes of God.

THE HEARTBREAKING COMPROMISE

There is a similar pattern emerging today. Many of our "Christian" homes are empty of prayer. Many of our children are growing up with more knowledge of the world than of the Word. We drop off our children at the church like laundry and want to pick up disciples of Christ when our own lives are more tuned in to *Monday Night Football* or *The Young and the Restless* than to the Spirit of the living God. The only time we open the Bible is on Sunday and the only time we use the name of Jesus is when we stub our toe.

We are not training our children to become warrior-priests for Christ. We are having prayer meetings for them to get into the fraternity or sorority that will help them climb the social ladder and get ahead. We are priding ourselves on their academic or athletic achievements while their souls are starving and their eternal destination is uncertain. While we have given them every material blessing their hearts have desired, we have robbed them of the pricelessness of self-sacrifice for a holy cause. We've created a well-dressed, socially-advanced, intellectually-articulate generation that is hungering for meaning, purpose and a sense of destiny. Our kids desperately need Jesus!

OUR FIRST NATION

A Church of the Nations mission begins in every home. Our first "nation" is those with whom we share our lives on a daily basis. If we accept the premise that every believer has a calling, then we need to begin now to train our children and youth in how to hear God's voice, how to seek His will, how to be saved and filled with the Holy Spirit.[14]

Our homes, from the single college student to the patriarchal grandfather, need to be focused on the ministry of discipleship. University roommates can have prayer and devotions, single moms can point hurting children to their Father God.[15] Dads can make worship and prayer a familiar family experience.[16] Grandparents can encourage scripture memorization.

Together we can remind ourselves that our purpose for being blessed is to be a blessing. Instilling in our families a divine sense of destiny and calling will do more to inoculate them against a corrupt world than all of our lectures and punishments.

Punishment is corrective, but calling a family to invest their lives in an eternal kingdom is preventive.

Our identity determines our behavior. If we view ourselves as being here to please ourselves and to live for our own enjoyment then we will act accordingly, but if we see ourselves as the one-of-a-kind creation of a personal God called to pursue Him, advance an eternal kingdom and build an overcoming church, then we will act to live meaning-filled and significant lives.[17]

Most youth are not rejecting the Church because the challenge is too demanding, they are rejecting the Church because the challenge is too small. They yearn to be a part of something full of adventure and purpose, but what do we communicate to them when we come to one service a week and never open the Bible in the home? What do they see in us that would communicate that the kingdom of God and the presence of Christ are the most exciting priorities in our lives?

The values we *portray* speak louder than the values we *proclaim*. How would the members of your family rate your priorities based on the amount of time, resource and energy you invest in each one? Is the pursuit of God the advancement of the Kingdom and the building of the Church on the list in their eyes? Is it happening in and through your home?

BEYOND BEING BORN AGAIN

In many cases, once a person gets saved and learns some basic discipleship, we don't really know what to do with them. Because we have become so focused on the blessings of salvation, we have lost the sense of mission. As a result, over time we start to slip back into the world's striving for success and meaning.

The church taught us that we needed to be saved and filled with the Holy Spirit, but then what? When we lose the call to yield to Christ and allow Him to touch a lost world through us, we lose the motivation to continue to learn to grow.

Our families go to church and continue their religious motions, but we don't remember why we do it anymore.[18] The habit is formed, but the hunger is lost. We know what we are supposed to do, we know how to do it, but we no longer know why. What a tragedy! Can we change the downward spiral?[19] How would your home be different if you and your children began to pray for the lost father of a child's playmate? What if the mailman became a family evangelistic project? Have you ever gone together to a nursing home to bless the lonely people who are trapped there or secretly raked a neighbor's leaves while they were on vacation? What would you communicate to your son if you started a Bible study for his little league baseball team? Or to your daughter if you took her with you on a mission trip to Mexico? Even a Christian tract left on the table after a meal communicates to your roommates or your kids that there is more to Christianity than getting saved and going to Heaven. There is a God to pursue, a kingdom to advance and a Church to build. The services of a Church of the Nations don't end when the building is emptied on Sunday morning, they have just begun.[20]

HOME-BASED FAITH

A Church of the Nations is a church made up of families. Single, blended or traditional, we are the one family of God called to be His expression in a dark world.

Our families must become our first field of focus as we awaken them to the ripened fields of harvest. Our families are the launching pad from which we send forth Christ's love. Our homes are the first sanctuaries our children will ever know and the family has the first responsibility before God for the instruction and training of the youth. The Church does not replace that responsibility, but supports it. The homes that we return to are our "Jerusalems" from which we can touch the "Judeas" and "Samarias" and the "uttermost parts of the Earth". When Christ and His kingdom are pursued in the home there is a great sense of adventure that is released in the lives of those who live there. Faith becomes more than a Sunday School experience. Faith becomes a lifestyle of joy and excitement as we learn to anticipate the Father's answers to prayer and watch for His activity all around us. Family-by-family a Church of the Nations joins together to become a living expression of Christ's love and acceptance, opening our arms to one another and to a desperately seeking world.

In an environment where so many come from broken families and painful childhood experiences our homes can become real centers of healing for the hurting. Many single believers, in need of a loving embrace and the model of a stable and caring home, could be nurtured into trust again if only one family would open their doors and their lives to them. A Church of the Nations must be a safe place for the wounded and bruised, a place where the masks and games of hide-and-seek are no longer played. Like one large family of faith, a Church of the Nations must become a place of love, acceptance and forgiveness for all who come sincerely to the Lordship of Christ and the calling of the kingdom. When a family is touched with the mission of Christ and reaches out to join with other families to fulfill that mission, then a Church of the Nations emerges that can truly touch the world for eternity. May our families be families with a mission as the strong bear the infirmities of the weak for the sake of Christ!

ENDNOTES

1   Matthew 16:26 "What good will it be for a man if he gains the whole world, yet forfeits his soul? Or what can a man give in exchange for his soul?"

2   I Timothy 5:8 If anyone does not provide for his relatives, and especially for his immediate family, he has denied the faith and is worse than an unbeliever.

3   I Timothy 3:4 & 7 "He must manage his own family well and see that his children obey him with proper respect....He must also have a good reputation with outsiders, so that he will not fall into disgrace and into the devil's trap.

4   1 Timothy 3:5 "If anyone does not know how to manage his own family, how can he take care of God's church?"

5   Genesis 2:18-22 The LORD God said, "It is not good for the man to be alone. I will make a helper suitable for him." Now the LORD God had formed out of the ground all the beasts of the field and all the birds of the air. He brought them to the man to see what he would name them; and whatever the man called each living creature, that was its name. So the man gave names to all the livestock, the birds of the air and all the beasts of the field. But for Adam no suitable helper was found. So the LORD God caused the man to fall into a deep sleep; and while he was sleeping, he took one of the man's ribs and closed up the place with flesh. Then the LORD God made a woman from the rib he had taken out of the man, and he brought her to the man.

6   Joshua 4:4-7 So Joshua called together the twelve men he had appointed from the Israelites, one from each tribe, and said to them, "Go over before the ark of the LORD your God into the middle of the Jordan. Each of you is to take up a stone on his shoulder, according to the number of the tribes of the Israelites, to serve as a sign among you. In the future, when your children ask you, `What do these stones mean?' tell them that the flow of the Jordan was cut off before the ark of the covenant of the LORD. When it crossed the Jordan, the waters of the Jordan were cut off. These stones are to be a memorial to the people of Israel forever."

7   Luke 2:21 On the eighth day, when it was time to circumcise him, he was named Jesus, the name the angel had given him before he had been conceived.

8 Luke 2:22-24 When the time of their purification according to the Law of Moses had been completed, Joseph and Mary took him to Jerusalem to present him to the Lord (as it is written in the Law of the Lord, "Every firstborn male is to be consecrated to the Lord"), and to offer a sacrifice in keeping with what is said in the Law of the Lord: "a pair of doves or two young pigeons."

9 Exodus 12:3 "Tell the whole community of Israel that on the tenth day of this month each man is to take a lamb for his family, one for each household."

10 Exodus 12:12-13 "On that same night I will pass through Egypt and strike down every firstborn — both men and animals — and I will bring judgment on all the gods of Egypt. I am the LORD. The blood will be a sign for you on the houses where you are; and when I see the blood, I will pass over you. No destructive plague will touch you when I strike Egypt.

11 Deuteronomy 4:10 Remember the day you stood before the LORD your God at Horeb, when he said to me, "Assemble the people before me to hear my words so that they may learn to revere me as long as they live in the land and may teach them to their children."

12 Psalm 78:56-58 But they put God to the test and rebelled against the Most High; they did not keep his statutes. Like their fathers they were disloyal and faithless, as unreliable as a faulty bow. They angered him with their high places; they aroused his jealousy with their idols.

13 Lamentations 1:5 Her foes have become her masters; her enemies are at ease. The LORD has brought her grief because of her many sins. Her children have gone into exile, captive before the foe.

14 Proverbs 22:6 "Train a child in the way he should go, and when he is old he will not turn from it."

15 Psalm 146:9 The LORD watches over the alien and sustains the fatherless and the widow, but he frustrates the ways of the wicked.

16 Ephesians 6:4 "Fathers, do not exasperate your children; instead, bring them up in the training and instruction of the Lord."

17 Romans 14:8 "If we live, we live to the Lord; and if we die, we die to the Lord. So, whether we live or die, we belong to the Lord."

18 Matthew 15:8-9 "`These people honor me with their lips, but their hearts are far from me. They worship me in vain; their teachings are but rules taught by men.'"

19 James 1:22-25 "Do not merely listen to the word, and so deceive yourselves. Do what it says. Anyone who listens to the word but does not do what it says is like a man who looks at his face in a mirror and, after looking at himself, goes away and immediately forgets what he looks like. But the man who looks intently into the perfect law that gives freedom, and continues to do this, not forgetting what he has heard, but doing it — he will be blessed in what he does."

20 James 1:26-27 "If anyone considers himself religious and yet does not keep a tight rein on his tongue, he deceives himself and his religion is worthless. Religion that God our Father accepts as pure and faultless is this: to look after orphans and widows in their distress and to keep oneself from being polluted by the world."

Relying on the Spirit

•••

The mission of the Church is not for us to win the world for Christ. The mission of the Church is for Christ to win the world through us.

Have you ever run out of gas? It is a frustrating feeling to be bound for a destination, cruising at top speed only to find yourself slowing to a stop miles from the nearest gas station.

Such is the fate of the person who goes out into the mission of Christ in their own strength and power. They end up on the side of the road, burned out, having exhausted all of their fuel.

Thumbs out, they'll soon be hitching a ride back home!

With all that has been said about the mission of Christ, the most important thing we can know is this: It is the *mission of Christ!* To say it clearly: it is *His* mission which must be done in *His* power and through *His* life if it is to succeed.

A MISPLACED FAITH

The greatest mistake we can make is to believe ourselves capable of sustaining the passion, power and focus necessary to become a Church of the Nations through our own willpower and resolve. The Father has not simply given us a mission and called us to accomplish it. He has given us something far more important: He has given us Himself. He has given us His life to indwell us and to be expressed through us. This life of Christ being expressed through the agency of our unique gifts and personalities is the only hope of the Church's success.

Christ in us is our hope of glory.

AN EARLY PASSION

As young believers, many of us start out with a tremendous zeal for Christ. We may come to the Lord out of backgrounds of brokenness and heartache; our own pain drives us into a life of sin and rebellion. By the time we hear and respond to the message of Christ, we are sickened by the confusion and suffering we have brought upon ourselves.

The first time we come to the cross, we come because of our sin. We know that we have sinned and we know that Christ has died for our sin. We confess our lost condition and receive Christ as our sin bearer and Savior.

We are so excited about this newfound peace that we make a determination. We determine to live for Christ. We will go where He says go and do what He says do. We will live like He says live and give what He says give.

We are totally committed. But notice the one small, but fatal flaw in our thinking. Who is it that is going to go, do, live and give? We are. I!

We are going to live our life for Christ. That is exactly what we do. For the next years of our life, we go out in the strength of our own life, always running close to empty and always giving everything we have for Jesus.

By the end of those years, we have achieved a great deal. We may have an envious reputation and ministry, but inside we are worn out, inauthentic, hollow and dry.

Our plastic facade is having a harder and harder time covering up our growing inner sense of treadmill Christianity. We are devoid of joy and slipping slowly into a kind of assembly-line ministry.

That's when we can suddenly find ourselves in an old familiar setting. We can find ourselves back at the cross.

A RETURN TO THE CROSS

The first time we came to the cross, we came because we were weary of our sin. The revelation we received there was that Christ had died on the cross for our sins, and there we were forgiven and cleansed.

But the second time we come to the cross, the issue is no longer sin. The issue is self.

The first time we learned that Christ died for us. The second trip to the cross, we learn that we died with Him.

"Know ye not that as many as were baptized into Christ Jesus were baptized into His death. We were buried with Him through baptism, so that just as Christ was raised from the dead, so you, too, should live a new life."[1] (KJV)

After years of living our lives for Christ, we may suddenly come to see a wondrous truth. God has made no provision for us to live our life for Christ.

Let me say it again: *God has made no provision for me to live my life for Christ.* The only provision the Father has made is for Christ to live His life through me.

The mission of the Church is not for us to win the world for Christ. The mission of the Church is for Christ to win the world through us.

As we cease our strivings and fleshly efforts to work for Christ, and instead learn to rest in His finished work on the cross, a transformation can take place in how we approach the ministry.

REDEFINING MINISTRY

Ministry can be redefined as yielding to His life within us and allowing Him to have full access to our giftings, aptitudes, resources and time for the accomplishment of His purposes. In essence, we are the branches and He is the vine.

Branches do not produce fruit. Branches merely bear — or temporarily hold — the fruit that the vine produces. In the same way, our definition of effective ministry is to yield our members to Christ as His instruments through which He can touch and heal a broken world. It is His mission. We are merely the vessels through which He operates to accomplish it.

Hammers do not hammer nails, carpenters do. A hammer merely yields to the carpenter's hand and surrenders to the use he makes of it.

Guitars do not play themselves. Without the hand of the musician, they are simply wood and string.

In the hands of the artist, a brush can paint masterpieces, apart from the artist, a brush can do nothing.

We are the tools, instruments and implements through which Jesus builds, plays and composes as He wishes. Apart from Him, we can do nothing. But through Him, all things become possible.

YIELDED VESSELS

A Church of the Nations is not made up of striving, guilt-ridden people driven to create programs and flesh-built systems in order to validate their worth and earn God's love and approval.

A Church of the Nations is learning to become a congregation of yielded vessels who have surrendered to the life of Christ within. They are seeking to cooperate with His desire to express Himself through them into a lost world.

Our fruitfulness in ministry is directly related to our depth of abiding in Christ. Out of that abiding relationship, like a branch to the vine, a flow of life is released. As the life-giving sap of the vine is released into the branch, fruit is produced. And as the fruit of His Spirit is released through our life, His fragrance will draw men unto Himself for healing and redemption.

Christ came to the Earth to redeem man. Today, He continues His ministry through us as we cease from our own self efforts and surrender to His will.

ENJOYING THE INHERITANCE

We are unconditionally loved by the Father. Our participation in the mission of the Church does not increase the Father's love and approval of us any more than our lack of involvement causes the Father's acceptance to decline.

We are not accepted because of what we do or do not do.

We are accepted because of what Christ has done. It is Christ in you that has made you accepted by the Father. If you are born of His Spirit, you are a beloved and eternal child of the Father.

There is nothing you can do to make God love you more and there is nothing you can do to make God love you less.

If we launch into a man-made ministry to the nations in our own strength in order to impress God or out of fear of His rejection, we will fail at our goals. It is not to be loved that we go as ambassadors, but because we are loved. It is not to obtain favor that we pursue His will, but because we have His favor. It is not to earn His acceptance that we yield to His life as instruments of righteousness, but because we are accepted in Christ .

We are free from using our lives to find approval. Because we don't need to use our life in order to obtain what has already been given to us freely in Christ, we are liberated from striving. We can relinquish control to His Spirit within and allow Him to work as He will within us.

HIS AMAZING GRACE

This unconditional love and acceptance of the Father is what fuels a Church of the Nations. It is His kindness that has led us to repentance, and it is His grace that has saved us.

More importantly, it is His grace that continues to sustain our every step as we learn to release the reins of our life to His Spirit and rest in His mighty power and strength.

Through His Holy Spirit in us, the wonderful gifts of the Spirit — faith, healing, miracles, words of wisdom and knowledge, spiritual language, interpretations and discernment — can become tools of ministry. By that same Spirit — love, joy, peace, patience, kindness, goodness, meekness, and self-control reflect the character of Christ's life expressed through us.

A Church of the Nations does not minister for Christ. A Church of the Nations allows Christ to minister through us. As John the Baptist once declared, *"He must increase, I must decrease."* This is the secret that has sustained the ministry of all of the Father's most effective and fruitful ministers.

A Church of the Nations never forgets that it is His mission to which we have been invited as vessels of His life. To the extent that we yield to His Holy Spirit and are filled with His presence, we will be useful instruments to display His power to the world.

A unified body of believers, yielded to His life within, can turn their world upside down.

Or rather, right side up.

Such is the vision of a Church of the Nations.

ENDNOTES

1   Romans 6:3-4 "Know ye not that as many as were baptized into Christ Jesus were baptized into His death. We were buried with Him through baptism, so that just as Christ was raised from the dead, so you, too, should live a new life." (KJV)

14

Fighting the Fight

•••

The seasoned warrior of Christ knows not to run at the first sign of resistance. Like David and Goliath, when the leading giant falls, all the other Philistines run away."

The one thing I was least prepared for when I entered the ministry was the amount of resistance I would encounter in the realm of the spirit.[1] I knew that the scriptures taught that we have an adversary who:

"—prowls around like a roaring lion looking for someone to devour."[2]

but I was somehow convinced that I could take on the kingdom of darkness and escape unscathed.

I NOW KNOW BETTER.

Any attempt to assault the gates of hell will result in victory for the persistent child of God.[3] But victories are not won without battles. And battles are not won without wounds.

The deeper our commitment to advance the kingdom of God, the greater threat we pose to the kingdom of darkness. The higher our threat level, the more intense the battles will be. The enemy will amass his troops, as any experienced commander would, where the greatest threat exists.

For the individual or church that decides to step out of the training camp and into the battlefield, there will be an instant and potentially debilitating level of spiritual attack.[4]

PREPARED FOR BATTLE

Often those who step out unprepared are so thrown by the resistance they initially encounter that they retreat back into the comfort zone of inactivity, forever cured of the desire to make an impact for Christ.

The enemy is clever. He knows that the persistent soldier of faith is bound by the Father's covenant to win the ultimate victory. To combat this, Satan releases a barrage of lies, deception and pressure. The first-time warrior thinks himself unable to continue to press the battle.

Little does the saint know that the enemy quickly runs out of ammunition because his one weapon is the weapon of lies and deception.[5] And the saint who knows the truth is already set free from his attacks.[6]

It is faith in the promises of God that shields us from the enemy's fiery darts,[7] and it is the sword of the Spirit (which is the Word of God) that assaults the enemy's strongholds and drives him out in defeat.[8]

The seasoned warrior of Christ knows not to run at the first sign of resistance. Like David and Goliath, when the leading giant falls, all the other Philistines run away.[9]

The advice of James to the church was:

Submit yourselves, then, to God. Resist the devil, and he will flee from you.[10]

But so often our experience is reversed. The Church raises its banner of assault, the enemy resists, and the Church runs away!

The church that decides to become a Church of the Nations will experience early and intense levels of resistance from many sides.

Households may experience physical attacks through attempts at sickness or injury. Businesses may experience financial assaults. And within every church there are a few tares sown among the wheat.[11] They are quick to stand up for doing nothing if the church decides to launch a major campaign towards reaching a lost world.

Never underestimate the enemy's creativity in finding ways to try and block the progress of any individual or church that seeks to step out of the crowd and take Christ at his Word.

But it helps to remember our history and biblical heritage. Have the great saints and patriarchs of old been heralded by the world as people of greatness,[12] or have they been more often ridiculed and resisted as people of scorn?

The book of Hebrews chapter eleven indicates that great victories are won by those who are willing to test their faith to its limit and to count the cost of following Christ.

The outcome is always glorious, but the journey is often difficult.

THE CENTRALITY OF THE CROSS

There is, in our day, a genuine admiration for and acceptance of a kind of "Cross-less Christianity" that costs the believer nothing and results only in greater and greater blessing for the individual devoted to practicing it. The commandments of the Lord do bring great blessing:

"Blessed is the man who fears the LORD, who finds great delight in his commands."[13]

Those who obey God's moral guidelines and cling to Biblical wisdom and instruction will surely be better off than they were when they followed their own counsel. But the prerequisites for discipleship defined by Christ himself were serious — and require complete surrender. Counting the cost is critical if we desire to fight through to the victory at the end of the inevitable struggles.[14]

It is not the promise of no struggle that compels us to follow Christ's will. Rather, it is the promise of final victory after the struggle. It is knowing that the struggle is for a Holy Cause that spurs us on to the goal.

If you are preparing for the active pursuit of God, advancement of His kingdom and building of His Church, then be equally prepared for the resistance of His enemy![15] Fight not in your own strength but in His strength and the power of His might. Take not the armor of Saul[16] but rather the sling-shot of faith and the Name of the Lord.

Let His final command "Go into all the world" drown out the voices that call you backward into comfort and triviality.

If as an individual or a church you are preparing to walk on the water, don't listen to the voices in the boat. "Boat-people" don't like "water-walkers." Never have; never will.

Listen to the one voice that counts. The voice of the one who walks in the midst of the stormy seas of a lost and dying world and bids you to come to him on the water.[17]

Once you've walked with Him on the waves, you'll never be satisfied in the boat again!

ENDNOTES

1 2 Corinthians 1:8 "We do not want you to be uninformed, brothers, about the hardships we suffered in the province of Asia. We were under great pressure, far beyond our ability to endure, so that we despaired even of life."

2 1 Peter 5:8b "—prowls around like a roaring lion looking for someone to devour."

3 2 Corinthians 2:14 "Now thanks be unto God, which always causeth us to triumph in Christ, and maketh manifest the savour of his knowledge by us in every place." (KJV)

4 1 Peter 4:12-13 Dear friends, do not be surprised at the painful trial you are suffering, as though something strange were happening to you. But rejoice that you participate in the sufferings of Christ, so that you may be overjoyed when his glory is revealed.

5 John 8:44b "—He was a murderer from the beginning, not holding to the truth, for there is no truth in him. When he lies, he speaks his native language, for he is a liar and the father of lies."

6 John 8:31-32 "Jesus said, "If you hold to my teaching, you are really my disciples. Then you will know the truth, and the truth will set you free."

7 Ephesians 6:16 "In addition to all this, take up the shield of faith, with which you can extinguish all the flaming arrows of the evil one."

8 2 Corinthians 10:4 "The weapons we fight with are not the weapons of the world. On the contrary, they have divine power to demolish strongholds."

9 1 Samuel 17:51 "David ran and stood over him. He took hold of the Philistine's sword and drew it from the scabbard. After he killed him, he cut off his head with the sword. When the Philistines saw that their hero was dead, they turned and ran."

10 James 4:7 Submit yourselves, then, to God. Resist the devil, and he will flee from you.

11 Matthew 13:25 "But while men slept, his enemy came and sowed tares among the wheat, and went his way." (KJV)

12 Hebrews 11:25-26 "He chose to be mistreated along with the people of God rather than to enjoy the pleasures of sin for a short time. He regarded disgrace for the sake of Christ as of greater value than the treasures of Egypt, because he was looking ahead to his reward."

1 Corinthians 4:10-13 "We are fools for Christ, but you are so wise in Christ! We are weak, but you are strong! You are honored, we are dishonored! To this very hour we go hungry and thirsty, we are in rags, we are brutally treated, we are homeless. We work hard with our own hands. When we are cursed, we bless; when we are persecuted, we endure it; when we are slandered, we answer kindly. Up to this moment we have become the scum of the earth, the refuse of the world. "

13 Psalm 112:1 "Blessed is the man who fears the LORD, who finds great delight in his commands."

14 Luke 14:28 "Suppose one of you wants to build a tower. Will he not first sit down and estimate the cost to see if he has enough money to complete it?"

15 1 Peter 4:1-2 "Therefore, since Christ suffered in his body, arm yourselves also with the same attitude, because he who has suffered in his body is done with sin. As a result, he does not live the rest of his earthly life for evil human desires, but rather for the will of God."

16 1 Samuel 17:38-40

17 Matthew 14:28-29 "Lord, if it's you," Peter replied, "tell me to come to you on the water." "Come," he said. Then Peter got down out of the boat, walked on the water and came toward Jesus.

How many beats of your heart remain? How many breaths before your last?

Only the Father knows.

How much of our present activity will have eternal value?

These are the most critical questions any person can ask.

Life is like a vapor. We are here today. We are gone tomorrow.

No one at death's door will say to themselves "I wish I had done less for Christ." No one will lament "I wish my participation in the Father's purposes had been scaled back."

But how many will remember wasted hours chasing after empty amusements while merely widening their own sense of inner thirst? *Everyone of us were fashioned in our mother's womb for a purpose[1].* Our members were written down in a book while we were being fashioned. Our days were recorded before even one of them was lived, and there were works ordained before time that the Father has planned for every one of us.

You are called of God. I say it unhesitatingly. You are His workmanship. You are ordained of God.

There is a great Mission which is the theme and backdrop to every event of human history. All of the universe leans over the rails of heaven to see the adventure unfold.

Don't miss the action. Don't give you strength to petty and insignificant things.

You are the Church! Be a Church of the Nations!

ENDNOTES

1   Psalm 139 13:16

CHURCH OF THE NATIONS
SCRIPTURAL BASIS: A PARTIAL LIST

Psalms 2:8	Ask of me, and I will make the NATIONS your inheritance, the ends of the earth your possession.
Psalms 9:11	Sing praises to the LORD, enthroned in Zion; proclaim among the NATIONS what he has done.
Psalms 18:47	He is the God who avenges me, who subdues NATIONS under me,
Psalms 18:49	Therefore I will praise you among the NATIONS, O LORD; I will sing praises to your name.
Psalms 22:27	All the ends of the earth will remember and turn to the LORD, and all the families of the NATIONS will bow down before him,
Psalms 22:28	for dominion belongs to the LORD and he rules over the NATIONS.
Psalms 45:5	Let your sharp arrows pierce the hearts of the king's enemies; let the NATIONS fall beneath your feet.
Psalms 45:17	I will perpetuate your memory through all generations; therefore the NATIONS will praise you for ever and ever.
Psalms 46:10	"Be still, and know that I am God; I will be exalted among the NATIONS, I will be exalted in the earth."
Psalms 47:1	For the director of music. Of the Sons of Korah. A psalm. Clap your hands, all you NATIONS; shout to God with cries of joy.
Psalms 47:3	He subdued NATIONS under us, peoples under our feet.
Psalms 47:8	God reigns over the NATIONS; God is seated on his holy throne.
Psalms 47:9	The nobles of the NATIONS assemble as the people of the God of Abraham, for the kings of the earth belong to God; he is greatly exalted.
Psalms 57:9	I will praise you, O Lord, among the NATIONS; I will sing of you among the peoples.

Psalms 67:2	that your ways may be known on earth, your salvation among all NATIONS.
Psalms 67:4	May the NATIONS be glad and sing for joy, for you rule the peoples justly and guide the NATIONS of the earth. Selah
Psalms 72:11	All kings will bow down to him and all NATIONS will serve him.
Psalms 72:17	May his name endure forever; may it continue as long as the sun. All NATIONS will be blessed through him, and they will call him blessed.
Psalms 82:8	Rise up, O God, judge the earth, for all the NATIONS are your inheritance.
Psalms 86:9	All the NATIONS you have made will come and worship before you, O Lord; they will bring glory to your name.
Psalms 96:3	Declare his glory among the NATIONS, his marvelous deeds among all peoples.
Psalms 96:7	Ascribe to the LORD, O families of NATIONS, ascribe to the LORD glory and strength.
Psalms 96:10	Say among the NATIONS, "The LORD reigns." The world is firmly established, it cannot be moved; he will judge the peoples with equity.
Psalms 98:2	The LORD has made his salvation known and revealed his righteousness to the NATIONS.
Psalms 99:1	The LORD reigns, let the NATIONS tremble; he sits enthroned between the cherubim, let the earth shake.
Psalms 99:2	Great is the LORD in Zion; he is exalted over all the NATIONS.
Psalms 102:15	The NATIONS will fear the name of the LORD, all the kings of the earth will revere your glory.
Psalms 105:1	Give thanks to the LORD, call on his name; make known among the NATIONS what he has done.
Psalms 105:44	he gave them the lands of the NATIONS, and they fell heir to what others had toiled for—
Psalms 106:47	Save us, O LORD our God, and gather us from the NATIONS, that we may give thanks to your holy name and glory in your praise.
Psalms 108:3	I will praise you, O LORD, among the NATIONS; I will sing of you among the peoples.

Psalms 111:6	He has shown his people the power of his works, giving them the lands of other NATIONS.
Psalms 113:4	The LORD is exalted over all the NATIONS, his glory above the heavens.
Psalms 117:1	Praise the LORD, all you NATIONS; extol him, all you peoples.
Psalms 126:2	Our mouths were filled with laughter, our tongues with songs of joy. Then it was said among the NATIONS, "The LORD has done great things for them."
Psalms 148:11	kings of the earth and all NATIONS, you princes and all rulers on earth,
Genesis 18:18	Abraham will surely become a great and powerful nation, and all NATIONS on earth will be blessed through him.
Genesis 22:18	and through your offspring all NATIONS on earth will be blessed, because you have obeyed me."
Genesis 26:4	I will make your descendants as numerous as the stars in the sky and will give them all these lands, and through your offspring all NATIONS on earth will be blessed,
Deuteronomy 15:6	For the LORD your God will bless you as he has promised, and you will lend to many NATIONS but will borrow from none. You will rule over many NATIONS but none will rule over you.
Deuteronomy 26:19	He has declared that he will set you in praise, fame and honor high above all the NATIONS he has made and that you will be a people holy to the LORD your God, as he promised.
Deuteronomy 28:1	If you fully obey the LORD your God and carefully follow all his commands I give you today, the LORD your God will set you high above all the NATIONS on earth.
Deuteronomy 28:12	The LORD will open the heavens, the storehouse of his bounty, to send rain on your land in season and to bless all the work of your hands. You will lend to many NATIONS but will borrow from none.
2 Samuel 8:11	King David dedicated these articles to the LORD, as he had done with the silver and gold from all the NATIONS he had subdued: 2 Samuel 22:48 He is the God who avenges me, who puts the NATIONS under me,
2 Samuel 22:50	Therefore I will praise you, O LORD, among the NATIONS; I will sing praises to your name.

1 Kings 4:34	Men of all NATIONS came to listen to Solomon's wisdom, sent by all the kings of the world, who had heard of his wisdom.
Matthew 12:18	18 "Here is my servant whom I have chosen, the one I love, in whom I delight; I will put my Spirit on him, and he will proclaim justice to the NATIONS.
Matthew 12:21	21 In his name the NATIONS will put their hope."
Matthew 24:14	14 And this gospel of the kingdom will be preached in the whole world as a testimony to all NATIONS, and then the end will come.
Matthew 24:30	30. "At that time the sign of the Son of Man will appear in the sky, and all the NATIONS of the earth will mourn. They will see the Son of Man coming on the clouds of the sky, with power and great glory.
Matthew 25:32	32 All the NATIONS will be gathered before him, and he will separate the people one from another as a shepherd separates the sheep from the goats.
Matthew 28:19	19 Therefore go and make disciples of all NATIONS, baptizing them in the name of the Father and of the Son and of the Holy Spirit,
Mark 11:17	17 And as he taught them, he said, "Is it not written: "`My house will be called a house of prayer for all NATIONS'? But you have made it `a den of robbers.'"
Mark 13:10	10 And the gospel must first be preached to all NATIONS.
Luke 24:47	47 and repentance and forgiveness of sins will be preached in his name to all NATIONS, beginning at Jerusalem.
Romans 4:17	17 As it is written: "I have made you a father of many NATIONS." He is our father in the sight of God, in whom he believed — the God who gives life to the dead and calls things that are not as though they were.
Romans 4:18	18. Against all hope, Abraham in hope believed and so became the father of many NATIONS, just as it had been said to him, "So shall your offspring be."
Romans 15:12	12 And again, Isaiah says, "The Root of Jesse will spring up, one who will arise to rule over the NATIONS; the Gentiles will hope in him."
Romans 16:26	26 but now revealed and made known through the prophetic writings by the command of the eternal God, so that all NATIONS might believe and obey him —

Galatians 3:8	8 The Scripture foresaw that God would justify the Gentiles by faith, and announced the gospel in advance to Abraham: "All NATIONS will be blessed through you."
1 Timothy 3:16	16 Beyond all question, the mystery of godliness is great: He appeared in a body, was vindicated by the Spirit, was seen by angels, was preached among the NATIONS, was believed on in the world, was taken up in glory.
Revelation 2:26	26. To him who overcomes and does my will to the end, I will give authority over the NATIONS —
Revelation 10:11	11 Then I was told, "You must prophesy again about many peoples, NATIONS, languages and kings."
Revelation 12:5	5 She gave birth to a son, a male child, who will rule all the NATIONS with an iron scepter. And her child was snatched up to God and to his throne.
Revelation 15:4	4 Who will not fear you, O Lord, and bring glory to your name? For you alone are holy. All NATIONS will come and worship before you, for your righteous acts have been revealed."
Revelation 19:15	15 Out of his mouth comes a sharp sword with which to strike down the NATIONS. "He will rule them with an iron scepter." He treads the winepress of the fury of the wrath of God Almighty.
Revelation 21:24	24 The NATIONS will walk by its light, and the kings of the earth will bring their splendor into it.
Revelation 21:26	26 The glory and honor of the NATIONS will be brought into it.
Revelation 22:2	2 down the middle of the great street of the city. On each side of the river stood the tree of life, bearing twelve crops of fruit, yielding its fruit every month. And the leaves of the tree are for the healing of the NATIONS.

Adopting an Unreached People

•••

There are several important steps to partnering with others in strategic outreach to those nations still untouched by the gospel. Obviously prayer is at the center of discovering God's purpose for any local congregation that would embark on such an adventure. For more information to assist your prayer efforts consider contacting one of the following sources:

U.S. Center for World Mission
1605 Elizabeth Street
Pasadena, CA 91104

AIMS
Box 64534
Virginia Beach, VA 23464

Adopt-A-People Clearinghouse
1539 East Howard Street
Pasadena, CA 91104

Frontiers
325 North Stapley Drive
Mesa, AZ 85203
Ph.# 1-800-GO2-THEM

RUN Ministries
(Reaching Unreached Nations)
P.O. Box 3312
Virginia Beach, VA 23454

I strongly encourage you to get the book OPERATION WORLD: A Day to Day Guide to Praying for the World by Patrick Johnstone available through your local Christian Bookstore.

Ask the Lord for a Nation as an Inheritance! He is a covenant keeping God!

BIBILIOGRAPHY

1. "Unveiled at Last", by Bob Sjogren, Published by YWAM Publishing, a ministry of Youth With a Mission; P.O. Box 55787, Seattle, WA 98155

2. "Operation World: The Day-by-day Guide to Praying for the World", by Patrick Johnstone. Published by Zondervan Publishing House, Grand Rapids, Michigan

3. "Lord Make My Life Count", by Raymond C. Ortlund. Published by Regal Books Division, G/L Publications; Glendale, CA 91209

4. The New International Version of the Bible, Copyright 1973, 1978, 1984 International Bible Society